Interracial America

OPPOSING VIEWPOINTS®

Other Books of Related Interest

Interracial America

O P P O S I N G   V I E W P O I N T S ®

Mary E. Williams, *Book Editor*

Bonnie Szumski, *Editorial Director*
Scott Barbour, *Managing Editor*

OPPOSING
VIEWPOINTS®
SERIES

Greenhaven Press, Inc., San Diego, California

Cover photo: Linda Tratechaud

Library of Congress Cataloging-in-Publication Data

Interracial America / Mary E. Williams, book editor.
    p.   cm. — (Opposing viewpoints series)
    Includes bibliographical references and index.
    ISBN 0-7377-0658-9 (lib. : alk. paper) —
ISBN 0-7377-0657-0 (pbk. : alk. paper)
    1. United States—Race relations. 2. United States—Ethnic
relations. 3. Ethnicity—United States. I. Williams, Mary E.,
1960–   II. Opposing viewpoints series (Unnumbered)

E184.A1 I595 2001
305.8'00973—dc21   00-066315
                                                          CIP

Greenhaven Press, Inc., P.O. Box 289009
San Diego, CA 92198-9009

"Congress shall make
no law...abridging the
freedom of speech, or of
the press."

First Amendment to the U.S. Constitution

The basic foundation of our democracy is the First
Amendment guarantee of freedom of expression.
The Opposing Viewpoints Series is dedicated to the
concept of this basic freedom and the idea that it is
more important to practice it than to enshrine it.

Contents

Why Consider Opposing Viewpoints?

*"The only way in which a human being can make some
approach to knowing the whole of a subject is by hearing
what can be said about it by persons of every variety of
opinion and studying all modes in which it can be looked
at by every character of mind. No wise man ever acquired
his wisdom in any mode but this."*

John Stuart Mill

In our media-intensive culture it is not difficult to find differing opinions. Thousands of newspapers and magazines
and dozens of radio and television talk shows resound with
differing points of view. The difficulty lies in deciding which
opinion to agree with and which "experts" seem the most
credible. The more inundated we become with differing
opinions and claims, the more essential it is to hone critical
reading and thinking skills to evaluate these ideas. Opposing
Viewpoints books address this problem directly by present-
ing stimulating debates that can be used to enhance and
teach these skills. The varied opinions contained in each
book examine many different aspects of a single issue. While
examining these conveniently edited opposing views, readers
can develop critical thinking skills such as the ability to
compare and contrast authors' credibility, facts, argumenta-
tion styles, use of persuasive techniques, and other stylistic
tools. In short, the Opposing Viewpoints Series is an ideal
way to attain the higher-level thinking and reading skills so
essential in a culture of diverse and contradictory opinions.

In addition to providing a tool for critical thinking, Opposing Viewpoints books challenge readers to question their
own strongly held opinions and assumptions. Most people
form their opinions on the basis of upbringing, peer pressure, and personal, cultural, or professional bias. By reading
carefully balanced opposing views, readers must directly confront new ideas as well as the opinions of those with whom
they disagree. This is not to simplistically argue that every-

one who reads opposing views will—or should—change his or her opinion. Instead, the series enhances readers' understanding of their own views by encouraging confrontation with opposing ideas. Careful examination of others' views can lead to the readers' understanding of the logical inconsistencies in their own opinions, perspective on why they hold an opinion, and the consideration of the possibility that their opinion requires further evaluation.

Evaluating Other Opinions

To ensure that this type of examination occurs, Opposing Viewpoints books present all types of opinions. Prominent spokespeople on different sides of each issue as well as well-known professionals from many disciplines challenge the reader. An additional goal of the series is to provide a forum for other, less known, or even unpopular viewpoints. The opinion of an ordinary person who has had to make the decision to cut off life support from a terminally ill relative, for example, may be just as valuable and provide just as much insight as a medical ethicist's professional opinion. The editors have two additional purposes in including these less known views. One, the editors encourage readers to respect others' opinions—even when not enhanced by professional credibility. It is only by reading or listening to and objectively evaluating others' ideas that one can determine whether they are worthy of consideration. Two, the inclusion of such viewpoints encourages the important critical thinking skill of objectively evaluating an author's credentials and bias. This evaluation will illuminate an author's reasons for taking a particular stance on an issue and will aid in readers' evaluation of the author's ideas.

It is our hope that these books will give readers a deeper understanding of the issues debated and an appreciation of the complexity of even seemingly simple issues when good and honest people disagree. This awareness is particularly important in a democratic society such as ours in which people enter into public debate to determine the common good. Those with whom one disagrees should not be regarded as enemies but rather as people whose views deserve careful examination and may shed light on one's own.

Thomas Jefferson once said that "difference of opinion leads to inquiry, and inquiry to truth." Jefferson, a broadly educated man, argued that "if a nation expects to be ignorant and free . . . it expects what never was and never will be." As individuals and as a nation, it is imperative that we consider the opinions of others and examine them with skill and discernment. The Opposing Viewpoints Series is intended to help readers achieve this goal.

Greenhaven Press anthologies primarily consist of previously published material taken from a variety of sources, including periodicals, books, scholarly journals, newspapers, government documents, and position papers from private and public organizations. These original sources are often edited for length and to ensure their accessibility for a young adult audience. The anthology editors also change the original titles of these works in order to clearly present the main thesis of each viewpoint and to explicitly indicate the opinion presented in the viewpoint. These alterations are made in consideration of both the reading and comprehension levels of a young adult audience. Every effort is made to ensure that Greenhaven Press accurately reflects the original intent of the authors included in this anthology.

Introduction

"The definitions of race and ethnicity have rarely been more fluid, the promise greater, the possible perils more pronounced."

—Newsweek, *September 18, 2000*

Satra Wasserman faced more than the usual difficulties as a child growing up in New York City. The son of a black mother and Jewish father, Wasserman attended a predominantly white school during the first grade, where he endured racial taunts almost every day. Children called him a "black cupcake" and told him, "Maybe if you took a bath, you'd be like us." In the fourth grade, after he had changed schools, he befriended a black classmate who invited him over to his house often. Wasserman relished this new friendship for about a year, until things suddenly changed: "Every time [my friend] asked his parents if I could come over, [their] answer was always no." It turned out that his friend's parents had discovered that Satra's father was white, and they no longer wanted him around their son.

The eighth grade, however, was Satra's most difficult year. While white students assumed he was black, his black peers teased him for being light-skinned and for having "Wasserman" as a last name. Since he did speak much of the slang that many of his black peers used, he was dubbed "Sir Oreo." ("Oreo" is an epithet used to describe blacks who allegedly "act white" or are "white on the inside.") To cope, Satra retreated into a world of baseball, video games, and comic books. Eventually, Satra claimed a biracial identity, realizing that "you just can't please everybody:"

> The biggest favor I did for myself was not trying to choose one race to be, which is a mistake most people in my situation make. The reason is that if I decided I was going to be black, first I'd be watching other people and imitating their image. Or, even worse, I would be watching TV or listening to music, trying to imitate the media's idea of blackness. And the same thing went for trying to be white. . . . Now I just do my own thing. I dress, talk, look, say and do what I want, the way I want. . . . It feels like I'm rebelling against the demons of my own past by just being myself.

Satra's experience reflects the lives of a growing number of youths in the United States. In the year 2000, marriages between people of different races and ethnicities numbered 1.3 million, and the estimated number of children born as a result of interracial relationships was three million and rising. In the past, many individuals who had parents of different races defined themselves monoracially, typically claiming to be the race of the darker-skinned parent. Today, however, an increasing number of mixed-race people are identifying themselves as multiracial.

In 1997, famous golfer Tiger Woods brought national attention to the issue of multiracial identity by revealing that he thought of himself as "Cablinasian"—a mixture of Caucasian, black, Indian, and Asian. Many African Americans initially disapproved of his claim to a mixed heritage, some arguing that he was trying to de-emphasize his blackness, others declaring that he was simply being naive. As one commentator quipped, "'Cablinasian' indeed. He'll wake up when somebody calls him the 'n' word."

This reaction to Woods' statement on his identity is best understood in the context of America's racial history—particularly black/white relations, which have dominated the legal and cultural battles surrounding race for much of the nation's existence. During slavery and up to the present day, people have usually been defined as black if they had any visible African features or ancestors of African descent. Known as the "one drop" rule, this kind of racial classification arose early in the nation's history to maintain a semblance of "separate" black and white races. In actuality, at least 70 percent of today's African Americans have Caucasian and/or Native American ancestry. However, a majority identify themselves as black rather than multiracial, largely because they realize that society generally perceives them as black. As one mother of biracial children explains, "My mixed-race children [are] Black—on their own and at their own peril, on the street, in school, in America, as they [look] at American history and into the mirror at the faces they [show] to the world." In addition, many African Americans affirm their blackness as an expression of solidarity and kinship with all those whom society defines as black.

Nevertheless, as America enters a new century, mixed-race people are gaining support in their affirmation of a multiracial identity. Some have called for the addition of a multiracial category on government, employment, and census forms that ask individuals to identify their race. In the opinion of multiracial activist G.L. Pettigrew, official recognition "paves the way for greater social and cultural acceptance of multiethnic people and interracial families. We highlight the absurdity of America's preoccupation with racial pigeon-holing, and perhaps together we can move this country closer to the day when race is no longer the highest issue." Organizations such as the National Association for the Advancement of Colored People, however, oppose such a category because they fear it could lead to an undercount of certain minority populations. As attorney Alan Jenkins argues, "Without reliable racial statistics, it would be virtually impossible for courts or agencies to detect institutional bias, and antidiscrimination laws would go unenforced." In his opinion, traditional monoracial categories—though arbitrary—remain necessary as long as racial discrimination exists.

In the year 2000, U.S. census forms first began allowing respondents to check more than one category under race and ethnicity. Although most people selecting this option will still be counted as minorities, many believe that this "multiple box" alternative heralds a refreshing willingness among Americans to explore the complexities of color and ethnicity. *Interracial America: Opposing Viewpoints* offers several perspectives on such issues in the following chapters: Should America's Racial Differences Be Emphasized? Will Immigration Lead to an Interracial Crisis? How Has Affirmative Action Affected Race Relations? How Should Society View Interracial Families? Representing various points on the political spectrum, the authors in this volume present compelling arguments on these culturally charged controversies.

CHAPTER 1

Should America's Racial Differences Be Emphasized?

Chapter Preface

America's population comprises many races and ethnicities, and the concept of "race" itself is complex. While it often seems easy to tell at first glance whether a person is white, black, or Asian, scientists point out that race has no biological basis. As geneticist Craig Venter explains, "Race is a social concept, not a scientific one. We all evolved in the last 100,000 years from the same small number of tribes that migrated out of Africa and colonized the world." External differences in skin color, he points out, reflect traits that developed over time due to environmental pressures: "Equatorial populations evolved dark skin . . . to protect against ultraviolet radiation, while people in northern latitudes evolved pale skin, the better to produce vitamin D from pale sunlight."

The concept of race, then, arose as a way to categorize the world's myriad ethnic and regional populations. Such categorization does more harm than good, many argue, as the notion of racial distinctions often intensifies divisiveness between and within ethnic groups. Some analysts believe that Americans should abandon racial categories altogether in order to promote social harmony. "Our . . . insistence on racial classification is insanity for a melting pot," argues columnist Paul Craig Roberts. "When it is more important to be 'black' or 'multiracial' than American, the concept of 'the public interest' is lost forever along with good will among citizens." Many others, however, maintain that race is a social reality that cannot be debunked at will. As writer Kenya Mayfield points out, "Clearly, there are racial inequities in this country, and it would be a mistake to 'sweep them under the carpet' by suddenly removing the word 'race' from our vocabulary."

The debate over the concept of racial categories is just one of the topics explored in the following chapter. Authors also examine the controversies surrounding ethnic diversity, integration, and racial pride.

> "How much 'diversity' can we tolerate
> before we cease to be one nation and one
> people?"

Racial and Ethnic Differences Endanger American Culture

Part I: Patrick Buchanan; Part II: Don Feder

In the following two-part viewpoint, syndicated columnists Patrick Buchanan and Don Feder contend that America is endangered by a growing population of nonwhite immigrants. In part I, Buchanan maintains that America will cease to be a cohesive nation if it continues to promote ethnic diversity and lenient immigration policies. A democracy cannot be sustained when its citizens have no common bonds, he asserts. In part II, Feder argues that the customs of many nonwhite immigrants are a threat to America's European-derived standards of liberty, justice, and responsibility. He claims that unless immigration is brought under control, America's traditional culture and identity will be destroyed.

As you read, consider the following questions:

1. In Buchanan's opinion, how is a nation defined?
2. According to Newt Gingrich, quoted by Buchanan, how many languages are spoken in the Chicago school system?
3. What percentage of new immigrants are nonwhite, according to Feder?

Part I: Reprinted from "How Much 'Diversity' Can America Tolerate?" by Pat Buchanan, *Conservative Chronicle*, August 20, 1997. Reprinted with permission from the author and Creators Syndicate. Part II: Reprinted from "Open Borders Shrink U.S. European Population," by Don Feder, *The Social Contract*, Summer 1998. Reprinted with permission from *The Social Contract*, Don Feder, and Creators Syndicate.

I

How did they get in? That question quickly came to mind on reading that two illegal aliens had been arrested in New York hours before they allegedly were going to blow themselves up, along with a few dozen unsuspecting commuters, at a subway station.

As for Ghazi Ibrahim Abu Maizar, we know how he got in. As Timothy Egan of the *New York Times* writes, he "followed a typical pattern for illegal immigrants. . . . He hiked into the Cascade Mountain woods from Canada [in 1996] and simply walked into the United States." Caught, he was sent back. He then strolled across the border again, was caught again and was tossed back again. Then, he rode in by bus, was arrested and requested asylum.

Why did he need asylum? Because, he said, the Israelis had him marked down as a terrorist, so he could not go home to the West Bank. How about going back to Canada? Nope, the Canadians refused to take him. So, the United States gave him 60 days to leave and turned him loose. He headed for New York. Of the border Abu Maizar crossed, Egan writes: "Whether this gateway between the populous Vancouver area in British Columbia and Seattle has become an entry point for terrorists or organized criminals remains an open question."

But is the question really open? Our government concedes that there are 5 million illegal aliens here. It is a near-certainty that enemies of this country have seeded that population with agents—for purposes of espionage, terror, assassination or reprisal.

A Threatened Nation

The *Times'* story of our unpoliced northwestern corridor raises the real question: Is America ceasing to be a nation?

A nation has been defined as a country of recognized borders, with people of common heritage, history, language, faith, culture, customs and heroes. That was the America we grew up in. We all spoke the same language, believed in the same concepts of right and wrong as taught in the Old and New Testaments, learned, whether in parochial or public school, the same glorious history. We listened to the same radio programs, went to the same movies, cheered the same heroes, celebrated the same holidays.

But the features that made Americans a distinct people, and the fences that made America separate, are disappearing. Ours are the most porous borders on Earth, though not porous enough for the *Wall Street Journal*, which champions a constitutional amendment to declare, "There shall be open borders!"

A Shrinking European Population

With 30 million immigrants since 1965, almost all now coming from Asia, Africa and Latin America, our European ethnic core—90 percent in 1965—is shrinking fast—to the delight of our president, who looks to the day soon when we are a nation of "minorities." We no longer worship the same God, share the same ideas of morality, admire the same heroes or celebrate the same holidays.

"Do you realize that there are 200 languages spoken in the Chicago school system? That's an asset, not a liability," Newt Gingrich recently burbled to Joe Klein. Oh. I thought the scattering of the peoples at the Tower of Babel, when the Lord confused their languages, was a punishment, not a blessing.

How much "diversity" can we tolerate before we cease to be one nation and one people? What do we have in common anymore?

"I am an American!" was once a boast every bit as proud as "Civis Romanus Sum!"—I am a citizen of Rome. In the early '60s, there was a debate over whether Churchill should be declared an honorary U.S. citizen; only Lafayette had been accorded the honor. Such was the reverence in which citizenship was held. In 1996, the Clintonites swore in 180,000 people as citizens, without even a check for a criminal record, so they could vote for Bill Clinton. Like the Lincoln bedroom, American citizenship has been cheapened.

Not to worry, we are told, we Americans are held together by a Constitution and a belief in democracy. But the quarrels over what the Constitution says—about gay rights, school prayer, abortion, quotas, the right to burn a flag—are the cause of our culture wars. As for a belief in democracy, is there anybody you know who would die to keep democracy alive in Marion Barry's Washington, D.C.?

"Providence has been pleased to give this one unconnected country to one united people . . . descended from the same ancestors, speaking the same language, professing the same religion, attached to the same principles of government, very similar in their manners and customs . . ." So exulted John Jay in The Federalist Papers, No. 2. Jay would today be charged with a hate crime against diversity.

II

America is slipping through our fingers. The America of the '50s, of my boyhood, is no more than a nostalgic memory. Twenty years hence, will the America of the 1990s seem idyllic compared to the murderous multicultural trailer park that then constitutes our disintegrating nation?

An Enriching Diversity?

It was one of those soft-news stories that *The New York Times* assumes will charm its readers but to which normal people react with less than elation.

"Ramadan Becomes an Extracurricular Subject," read the headline. "As new immigrants swell the numbers of Muslims in New York City, the rites of . . . Islam's holiest period have quietly seeped into the culture of the city's schools."

At John Jay High School, administrators announce the onset of Ramadan on the public address system. Apparently it is only official recognition of *Western* religion that threatens church-state separation.

"Islam is said to be the fastest-growing faith in America," the *Times* discloses.

How we are enriched by the quaint customs of newcomers! On March 29, 1997, a little publicized federal law will go into effect that criminalizes the practice of genital mutilation of women under 18, a practice prevalent in 28 African nations. According to the Centers for Disease Control, there are 150,000 girls and women of African descent in this country who have been or are in danger of being so maimed.

In Lincoln, Nebraska, two Iraqis are under arrest for marrying sisters, ages 13 and 14. An account in *Newsweek* notes such marriages are common in Moslem countries. Since we are informed that America must now adapt to immigrants (instead of the reverse), perhaps we should abolish our culturally insensitive laws against statutory rape.

More than 50,000 members of the Caribbean Santeria cult have immigrated to South Florida, where they are enhancing the state's diversity by sacrificing chickens, goats and other small animals to voodoo rituals.

The Dangers of Non-White Immigration

Whenever I write about immigration, indignant communications pour in accusing me of stigmatizing today's immigrants in the same way that my xenophobic precursors degraded and dehumanized earlier waves of Irish, Italian and Jewish immigrants.

Equating immigrants of the 1890s and the 1990s is a soothing myth. The old immigrants actually had things in common with the American majority of their day.

A Fact of Human Nature

People prefer to live and deal with their own kind, in their own culture. This has always been true—everywhere. No amount of Politically Correct posturing or celebrating of diversity has ever changed this fact of human nature. Note that while ethnicity may involve racial and other visible characteristics, this is not always or necessarily the case, and certainly does not explain all. A feeling of ethnic or national identity can cross racial and descent lines, if the prevailing culture is healthy and confident. Multiethnic, multicultural, multinational societies strongly tend to split apart, though on the surface they may be held together for some time by a strong, often repressively authoritarian regime. During a buildup of ethnic tensions many people, though perhaps growing increasingly uneasy in a vague way, are often unaware of the significance of events taking place before their eyes.

Lee G. Madland, *Social Contract*, Spring 2000.

The aforementioned groups were European. Two were Christian; the third practiced the religion from which Christianity sprang. All came from societies that respected law and had common concepts of justice, liberty and individual responsibility.

The Jews gave the world the Bible. Irish monks preserved Western civilization during the Dark Ages. Italy was the embodiment of the Renaissance.

Over 90 percent of new immigrants are non-white. Many come from caudillo cultures where corruption is pervasive. Most have a *mañana* work ethic. Their customs and traditions are as alien to our own as sushi to kosher cuisine.

Increasingly, they see themselves as a bloc (people of color—pink doesn't count) arrayed against white Americans. In California in 1996, Asians—our model minority—voted by a 55 percent margin to maintain the state's system of anti-white discrimination.

Due in large part to our open-borders style of national suicide, America's European population will shrink from 73.6 percent today to 52.8 percent in 2050.

What kind of America will your children and grandchildren inherit—the multiculturalists' delusion of Diversity Disney World where a rainbow of smiling faces celebrates their differences, or Rwanda with high-tech machetes?

I'd rather read about voodoo rites than have my next-door neighbors practice them. I'll willingly forego more ethnic restaurants for telephone operators who speak my language. The knowledge that America's fastest-growing religion is one that oppresses all others wherever it achieves power does not comfort me.

In 1993, the Sierra Club published a coffee-table book called *Endangered Peoples* covering such exotic topics as the Tuareg of North Africa and the Amazon's Yanomami tribe.

Neglected is a group on the brink of extinction that actually made a contribution to civilization—the Americans. As for the Tuareg and Yanomami, they'll all be here a few years.

*"We came in different ships, but we now
ride in the same boat."*

Racial and Ethnic Differences
Are Not Dangerous

Amitai Etzioni

America is not endangered by its population's racial and ethnic differences, asserts Amitai Etzioni in the following viewpoint. For one thing, he points out, minorities' values generally do not oppose those of the white majority. More often
than not, Americans of various backgrounds hold similar
opinions on social and political issues, writes Etzioni. While
racial minorities and immigrants may uphold some ethnic and
national traditions, they generally share with white Americans
a commitment to democracy, hard work, and tolerance. Etzioni is a professor at George Washington University and the
editor of the quarterly journal *Responsive Community*.

As you read, consider the following questions:
1. According to Etzioni, what percentage of marriages in
   1995 were interracial or interethnic?
2. What is problematic about the phrase "Asian-American,"
   in the author's opinion?
3. According to a 1994 survey cited by Etzioni, what
   percentage of blacks believes that hard work is the way to
   get ahead? What percentage of whites?

Reprinted from "A Nation of Minorities?" by Amitai Etzioni, *Responsive
Community*, Winter 1999/2000. Reprinted with permission from the author. A
much more extensive discussion of this topic can be found in *The Monochrome
Society*, to be published in Spring 2001 by Princeton University Press.

The young CEO felt strongly that "soon all America will look like California" and that we must prepare ourselves, employees, and fellow citizens for life in a diverse, "multicultural" America. The occasion was a "sensitivity" training workshop, which seeks to teach managers how to prepare their underlings to deal with people of different social backgrounds.

The CEO's demographic acumen was quite keen. Much of America, and not only California, is being diversified. A growing number of immigrants from Latin America and Asia are settling in communities far away from both the Mexican border and the Pacific coast, in places such as Wausau, Wisconsin and Storm Lake, Iowa. This population movement has led some commentators to argue that America in the foreseeable future will become a country in which European-Americans are a minority and Americans of other ethnic and racial backgrounds are the majority. Demographer Martha Farnsworth Riche wrote an article for the prestigious *American Demographics* entitled, "We're All Minorities Now," stating that "the United States is undergoing a new demographic transition: it is becoming a multicultural society. . . . [Soon] it will shift from a society dominated by whites and rooted in Western culture to a world society characterized by three large racial and ethnic minorities." A special issue of *Time* magazine dedicated to envisioning our ethnic future declared that ". . . America is moving toward an era when there may be no ethnic majority, with whites just another minority."

Such visions of America are belied by elementary statistics. If the present trends continue, there will be a white majority in the United States for at least a whole generation and longer. For instance, by the year 2030 whites will still constitute 60.5 percent of all Americans, hardly a minority. Over more than a generation, from 1995 to 2030, the proportion of blacks in the population is expected to increase by a mere 1.1 percent and that of Asians by 3.3 percent. The increase in the Hispanic population in the same time period is believed to be much heftier: a substantial 8.7 percent. Still, all said and done, the share of the non-Anglo population would grow—over 35 years—by not more than 13.1 percent.

Those who venture still deeper into the future, disregarding that such long-run predictions are often woefully off the mark, still foresee a white majority (albeit barely so) in the faraway year 2050. Regardless, such analysis misses the point. *The main question is not what the pigmentation of future Americans will be, but how they will relate to one another.*

A New Amalgam

One fact, often overlooked in this context, is that as America steams forward, far from being more splintered along racial and ethnic lines, surprisingly strong bonds of intermarriage are evolving, which bridge the divisions that diversity advocates like to sharpen. (In earlier ages, people were inclined to tolerate working with and living next to people of different backgrounds, but were troubled when their children married a person from a different racial or ethnic background. These feelings have not disappeared, but have weakened considerably.) One out of 12 marriages in 1995 (8.4 percent) were interracial/ethnic marriages. Intermarriage between Asian-Americans and whites are particularly common, and marriages between Hispanic-Americans and whites are also rather frequent, while such marriages with African-Americans are the least common. All in all, intermarriages of all kinds are on the rise. Since 1970, the proportion of marriages among people of different racial or ethnic origin has increased by 72 percent and is expected to rise in the future.

That is, while there may well be more Americans of non-European origin, a growing number of the American white majority will have a Hispanic daughter or son-in-law, an Asian stepfather or mother, and a whole rainbow of cousins. Sociologists stress that such intermarriages are of special importance for community building precisely because they create particularly intimate bonds not merely for the married couple but also for their extended families.

What Is Latino? Who Is Asian?

The very notion that there are social groups called "Asian-Americans" or "Latinos" is a statistical artifact reflecting the way social data are coded and reported. The notion is promoted by ethnic leaders who have anointed themselves to speak for (and to try to fashion and perpetuate) distinct social groups, and is a shorthand the media finds convenient. Most of the so-called Asian-Americans do not see themselves as, well, Asian-Americans, and many resent being labeled this way. Many Japanese-Americans do not feel a particular affinity to Filipinos or Pakistani-Americans, or to Korean-Americans. And the feelings are reciprocal. Paul Watanabe, of the Institute for Asian American Studies at the University of Massachusetts, himself an American of Japanese descent, remarks, "There's this concept that all Asians are alike, that they have the same history, the same language, the same background. Nothing could be more incorrect."

Most Americans of Asian heritage would rather be identified by the country of their origin. Setsuko Buckley, a Japanese language teacher at Western Washington University, points out that, "Asian-Americans need to be divided into Japanese-Americans or Chinese-Americans or Korean-Americans—just because they want to be. Even Southeast Asians are different from each other—Vietnamese, Thai, Cambodian—and they should have the option of being called what they want." On the other side of the continent, the social categories are not any different. A study of a New York City high school, conducted by Queens College sociologist Pyong Gap Min, found that most young Americans of Korean origin do not consider themselves Asian-American but Korean-American.

William Westerman of the International Institute of New Jersey complains about Americans who tend to ignore the cultural differences among Asian nations, which reflect thousands of years of tradition. He wonders how the citizens of the United States, Canada, and Mexico who move to Europe would feel if they were all treated as indistinguishable "North Americans."

The same holds for the so-called Latinos, including three of my sons. Americans of Hispanic origin trace their origins to many different countries and cultures. Eduardo Diaz, a social-service administrator puts it this way: "[T]here is no place called Hispanica. I think it's degrading to be called something that doesn't exist." A Mexican-American office worker remarked that when she is called Latina it makes her think "about some kind of island." Many Americans from Central America think of themselves as "mestizo," a term that refers to a mixture of Indian and European ancestry. Among those surveyed in the National Latino Political Survey in 1989, the greatest number of respondents chose to be labeled by their country of origin, as opposed to pan-ethnic terms such as "Hispanic" or "Latino."

The significance of these and other such data is that far from dividing the country into two or three hardened minority camps, we are witnessing an extension of a traditional American picture: Americans of different origins identifying with groups of other Americans from the same country—at least for a while—but not with any large or more lasting group.

Multiculturalism or American Creed?

Above all, it is a serious mistake to believe that because American faces may appear a bit more diverse a generation from now (if one goes by skin color or the shape of one's eyes) that most Americans of different social backgrounds will follow a different agenda or hold a different creed than the white majority. For example, a 1992 survey found that although most Americans (79 percent) favor "fair treatment for all, without prejudice or discrimination," the numbers for blacks and Hispanics are even higher (86 percent and 85 percent, respectively). Similarly, a poll of New York City residents shows that the vast majority of respondents considered teaching "the common heritage and values that we share as Americans" to be "very important." Again, minorities endorse this position even more so than whites: 70 percent of whites compared with 88 percent of Hispanics and 89 percent of blacks.

On numerous issues the differences among various Hispanic groups are as big or bigger than between these groups and "Anglo" Americans. A study by Louis DeSipio found that while 42 percent of Cubans and 51 percent of Anglos agreed with the statement that US citizens should be hired over noncitizens, 55 percent of Puerto Ricans and 54.7 percent of Mexicans adopted the same position. Quotas for jobs and college admissions were favored only by a minority of any of these four groups studied, but Cubans differed from Mexicans and Puerto Ricans more (by 14 percent) than from whites (by 12 percent).

The fact that various minorities do not share a uniform view, which could lead them to march lock-step with other minorities to a new America (as some on the left fantasize) is also reflected in elections. Cuban-Americans tend to vote Republican, while other Americans of Hispanic origin are more likely to vote Democratic. Americans of Asian origin cannot be counted on to vote one way or another, either. For instance, of the Filipino-Americans registered to vote, 40 percent list themselves as Democrats, 38 percent as Republicans, and 17 percent as independent. First-generation Vietnamese-Americans tend to be strong anti-Communists and favor the Republican party, while older Japanese- and Chinese-Americans are more often Democrats.

The Benefits of Mutuality and Tolerance

Mutuality is distinct from tolerance, which is a live-and-let-live concept that requires distance, sometimes privacy. Mutuality demands active engagement, learning about others in their own terms—not a suspension of judgment, but judgment based on information and interaction. Tolerance is a politics of peaceful coexistence; mutuality is a politics of recognition. . . .

But we need to stop short of the strong multiculturalism that proclaims "permanent group distinctions." A second perspective must come into play: a principle of permeability, which insists on both the reality of group boundaries and the ability to cross them. An exclusively descent-based theory of group identity is no longer tenable.

Alexander T. Aleinikoff, *American Prospect*, January/February 1998.

We often encounter the future first in California. In a 1991 Los Angeles election for the California State Assembly, Korean-American, Filipino-American, and Japanese-American candidates ran, splitting the so-called "Asian-American" vote, not deterred by the fact that they ensured the election of a white candidate. Candidates of all kinds of backgrounds may carry the day in twenty-first century America, but the notion that all minorities, or even most members of any one minority, will line up behind them, is far from a safe bet.

A Growing Black Middle Class

While African-Americans are clearly the least mainstreaming group, there is a growing black middle class, many members of which have adopted rather similar life styles and aspirations to other middle-class Americans. Even if one takes all African-Americans as a group, one could be swayed too far by the data on the great differences in the ways whites and blacks perceived the O.J. Simpson trial and other matters directly concerning racial issues. When it comes to basic tenets of the American creed, the overwhelming majority of blacks strongly accept them. For instance, a national survey asked in 1994: "a basic American belief has been that if you work hard you can get ahead—reach your goals and get more." Sixty-seven percent of blacks responded "yes, still true," only ten percent less than whites. Most blacks (77 percent) say they prefer equality of opportunity to equality of results (compared to 89 percent of whites). When it comes to "do you see yourself as traditional or old-fashioned on things such as sex, morality, family life, and religion, or not," the difference between blacks and whites was only 5 percent, and when asked whether values in America are seriously declining, the difference was down to one percentage point. Roughly the same percentages of blacks and whites strongly advocate balancing the budget, cutting personal income taxes, and reforming Medicare. Percentages are also nearly even in responses to questions on abortion and marijuana.

In an extensive national survey, conducted at the University of Virginia, James Davison Hunter and Carl Bowman found that ". . . the majority of Americans do not engage in identity politics—a politics that insists that opinion is mainly a function of racial, ethnic, or gender identity or identities rooted in sexual preference." While there were some disagreements on specific issues and policies, this study found more similarities than discrepancies. Even when asked about such divisive issues as the direction of changes in race and ethnic relations, the similarities across lines were considerable. Thirty-two percent of blacks, 37 percent of Hispanics and 40 percent of whites feel these relations are holding steady; 36 percent, 53 percent, and 44 percent feel they have declined, respectively. (The rest feel that they have improved.) That is, on most issues, four out of five Americans—or more!—agreed with one another, while those who differed amounted to less than 20 percent. No anti-anything majority here.

A Community of Communities

All this does not mean that diversity is a figment of the overblown imagination of a bunch of left-liberals and small bands of political leaders. But the changes in America's demographics do not imply that the American creed is being or will be replaced by something called "multiculturalism." The American creed always had room for pluralism of *sub*-cultures, of people upholding some of the traditions and values of their countries of origin, from praying to playing in their own way. But this pluralism was, is, and must be one that is bounded by a shared framework if America is to be spared the kind of ethnic tribalism that tears apart countries as different as Yugoslavia and Rwanda, and raises its ugly head even in well-established democracies such as Canada and the UK.

Which social, cultural, and legal elements constitute the framework that holds together the diverse mosaic? A commitment by all parties to the democratic way of life, to the Constitution and its Bill of Rights, and to mutual tolerance. It is further fortified by a strong conviction that one's station in life is determined by hard work and saving, by taking responsibility for one's self and one's family. And most Americans still share a strong sense that while we are different in some ways, in more ways we are joined by the shared responsibilities of providing a good society for our children and ourselves—one free of racial and ethnic strife—and providing the world with a model of a country whose economy and polity are thriving. Indeed, we came in different ships, but we now ride in the same boat.

*"Our government's insistence on racial
classification is insanity for a melting pot."*

Racial Classifications Should Be Abandoned

Part I: Deroy Murdock; Part II: Paul Craig Roberts

The authors of the following two-part viewpoint contend
that the U.S. government's system of racial classification
should be abandoned. In part I, cable news commentator
Deroy Murdock argues that racial classifications are harmful
because they place group identity over individual rights.
People should be esteemed for their unique character and
abilities, not for their pigmentation, Murdock writes. In part
II, columnist Paul Craig Roberts charges that racial categories reflect the interests of political groups who wish to
promote unfair preferences based on race and ethnicity. In
the end, Roberts maintains, such categories undermine
America's melting-pot ideals.

As you read, consider the following questions:

1. According to Murdock, how did the Suffolk County
   Police Department attempt to correct its shortage of
   black and Hispanic officers?
2. According to Roberts, which groups opposed the
   addition of a "multiracial" category to the government's
   racial classification system?
3. Why did an Egyptian immigrant sue to have his racial
   classification changed from "white" to "black," in
   Roberts's opinion?

I

The road to color blindness is as colorful as ever. Recent court decisions and ballot measures should cheer those who want government to stop fretting about its citizens' pigmentation. Nonetheless, evidence abounds that bureaucrats remain enamored of racial calculus.

Take the Seattle Public School District. It requires potential employees, contractors and vendors to complete a form that seems to have been written by curators at an anthropology museum. It's designed to foster "an ethnic configuration, both male and female, that reflects the multiracial characteristics of the student population."

The form instructs applicants to "select from below the one most appropriate racial/ethnic group with which you choose to be identified." It then offers 18 different "permissible codes" each beside a check-off box. These racial labels include that perennial favorite, "White," grouped with "Gypsy." The latter is defined tautologically as "a person having origins in the original Gypsy groups of Europe." Other codes include "Alaskan Native," "East Indian" (covering those from India, Ceylon and, "in some cases, Pakistan") and "Latino White" which involves Latinos with roots in "North Africa, the Middle East or the Indian subcontinent." Perhaps Seattle offers a support group for Latino-Middle-Eastern-Americans.

This document slides from the silly to the sinister when applicants refuse to be shoehorned into these boxes. They may describe their ethnicity in the comment section. Then, the form explains, "a member of the Personnel Department will assign one of the racial/ethnic codes to you based on his or her best judgment."

There's a whiff of Nuremberg about all this. The notion of public employees subjecting job applicants to racial inspections should give Americans goose bumps. So it goes when government substitutes group identity for individual equality before the law.

Racial Politics

Something similar is afoot on Long Island, N.Y., where public safety has fallen hostage to racial politics. The 2,900-member

Suffolk County Police Department, or SCPD, historically has had few blacks and Hispanics. It could have addressed this issue color-blindly, namely through active minority outreach and recruiting. Instead, it created a minority-only cadet program whose members merely needed a passing score of 70 on the police academy entrance exam to be admitted, rather than "in the high 90s" for whites, according to SCPD spokesman Officer Robert Boden.

It's bad enough that Suffolk degraded blacks and Hispanics by assuming they couldn't ace the test. One top cop has been suspended and another officer and a retiree have been indicted by Suffolk district attorney James Catterson for possibly giving some of these cadets improper tutoring before a 1996 test. Meanwhile, four white males and a part-black female, who says she looks white, sued when they were barred as cadets for being Caucasian. Federal District Judge Joanna Seybert rejected the program as unconstitutional. Suffolk County may appeal.

A Noxious Stew

Back on the West Coast, language and race have been blended in a noxious stew. In Oakland, Calif., birthplace of ebonics, George Louie is battling educrats about their treatment of his 5-year-old son, Travell De Shawn Louie.

Travell is black and only speaks English. Yet, without parental notice, he was placed in a bilingual kindergarten classroom in which the kids were taught in Cantonese. Louie complained to the principal, who wouldn't place Travell in an English-only class. Eventually the child was moved to a classroom in which he is taught in English geared toward Chinese-speakers. Why is Travell in a Chinese-oriented class? Follow the money. Transferring him to an English-speaking class would cost the school the subsidies it receives for each bilingual student.

Louie is suing the Oakland schools with the help of the Center for Equal Opportunity, or CEO, in Washington. As CEO's Jorge Amsell puts it: "The school is taking a child who speaks English, creating a language barrier and then not serving his needs."

If passed, California's "English for the Children" initiative will dump such bilingual nonsense. In November 1998, voters to the north could ditch those racial boxes for good by passing the Washington Civil Rights Initiative. [In June 1998, California voters passed an initiative that ended bilingual education programs in that state. The Washington Civil Rights initiative, which bans public education preferences based on race, ethnicity, and gender, passed in November 1998].

A nation enslaved.

Mike Ramirez. Reprinted with permission from Copley News Service.

Americans could learn a lesson from Russia. As E.V. Kontorovich reported in the *Wall Street Journal*, in 1997, the Kremlin stopped identifying its citizens as members of the Tatar, Chukchi and 101 other ethnic categories. National ID cards now let Russians be Russians.

In 1963, the Rev. Martin Luther King Jr. dreamed aloud about a place where his children would be judged by the content of their character, not the color of their skin. As with Sputnik, it looks like Russia got there first.

II

In the 1990 census, 10 million Americans could not fit themselves into the federal government's racial classification system and checked "other." For the past several years, the government has been studying how to adjust its racial classification to accommodate the 10 million "others." An obvious solution was "multiracial," but this category was opposed by organized racial interest groups that benefit from employment quotas and contract set-asides. These groups argued that the multiracial category would dilute their numbers and corresponding political clout.

The racial spoils system prevailed. The government refused to add "multiracial" to its list but will permit "others" to define themselves by checking multiple boxes. For example, a person with parents and grandparents from different classifications can check each box on the form and be identified as "white, Asian, African-American" or "Pacific Islander, white, American Indian."

Acting Assistant Attorney General for Civil Rights Isabelle Katz Pinzler says that for purposes of the racial spoils system, the government will designate the race of those who chose multiple classification. A "white, Asian, African-American" will be counted as black. This pleases the organized racial groups, because their numbers will now expand by 10 million.

Multiracial spokespersons, however, are unhappy. They correctly perceive that the decision has denied them the opportunity "to gain recognition and an identity as a group." The importance of group identity as opposed to American identity is apparent from the multiracials' defeat. Black and Latino interest groups got their way because polls show they voted overwhelmingly for President Bill Clinton. Multiracials could make no such claim. Lacking official recognition, they are not polled as a group and are thus deprived of a group voice.

Racial Nonsense

Recently, an Egyptian immigrant to the United States was outraged to discover that despite the blackness of his skin, he was officially classified as "white" for racial purposes because the federal government in its wisdom has determined that Egyptians are "white." He is suing to have his classification changed to "black" in order to benefit from the racial preferences that reward skin color.

The Egyptian immigrant's case illustrates the problem

with every racial classification system. The U.S. system is exclusive and reflects the arbitrary interests of organized political groups. On its face, the classification is nonsense. America has many ethnic groups, but Hispanic is the only ethnic option listed. Moreover, there are no such races as white, black and Asian. There are as many differences between English and Italians, Spaniards and Germans, and French and Russians as there are between a Masai and an Ibo, a Hausa and a Zulu, a Chinese and a Japanese.

Historically, European nations have experienced far more conflict among themselves than they have had with blacks, and the genocidal conflicts among African tribes greatly overshadow any black-white antagonisms. Anyone who polls Koreans and Chinese will find a hatred of Japanese, not of white Americans who allegedly discriminate against them. Little doubt, there are still Britishers today who do not hesitate to hire a black from Rhodesia, an Indian or a Hong Kongese but balk at hiring a Frenchman.

Some years ago on an anniversary of the atomic bombing of Hiroshima, a young TV newswoman was soliciting live opinions from New Yorkers on America's perfidy when she spied an Asian woman. Not knowing the Asian races, she pushed the microphone in the face of a Korean female, who promptly deflated the exercise by responding that the Americans had not dropped enough nuclear bombs on Japan.

An Impossible Task

Our government's insistence on racial classification is insanity for a melting pot. When it is more important to be "black" or "multiracial" than American, the concept of "the public interest" is lost forever along with goodwill among citizens.

That is an extraordinary cost to pay for the impossible task of unscrambling the human omelet. In a 1980 racial preferences case, Justice John Paul Stevens predicted: "If the national government is to make a serious effort to define racial classes by criteria that be administered objectively, its study precedents such as the First Regulation to the Reich Citizenship Law of Nov. 14, 1935."

Stevens correctly recognized the implication of America's racial preferences, but not even National Socialism's bureaucrats could sort out the ambiguities of family trees. South Africa, like the United States today, tried to organize society and law according to racial classification, but its parliament was forced to amend the 1950 Population Registration Act seven times because of unforeseen complications.

Perhaps the United States will succeed where Apartheid and the Nazis failed. But it is going to be a long, hard struggle. The last several years produced no breakthrough. The more promising approach is to abandon racial classification.

> *"Reliable racial data are crucial to enforcing our basic laws against intentional racial discrimination, which enjoy broad public support."*

Racial Classifications Should Not Be Abandoned

Alan Jenkins

The use of racial categories should not be abolished, contends Alan Jenkins in the following viewpoint. He maintains that racial data collection provides the tools necessary to identify racial bias when it occurs. Racial statistics have, for example, helped to uncover patterns of discrimination in housing, employment, law enforcement, and health care. Civil rights laws would be impossible to enforce without accurate racial data, Jenkins points out. Moreover, America would not be able to track its progress in conquering racial discrimination without reliable information about the opportunities that are available to different racial groups. Jenkins, a former Justice Department attorney, is a program officer for Human Rights and International Cooperation at the Ford Foundation.

As you read, consider the following questions:
1. According to studies cited by the author, how often do Latinos and African Americans encounter discrimination when seeking to purchase a home?
2. What percentage of surveyed whites believes that blacks do not face discrimination in housing or employment, according to Jenkins?

Excerpted from "See No Evil," by Alan Jenkins, *The Nation*, June 28, 1999. Reprinted with permission from the June 28, 1999, issue of *The Nation*.

The affirmative action wars have claimed another victim: the truth. Having scored victories in California, Washington and Texas—as well as setbacks in Congress and state legislatures around the country—opponents of affirmative action have set their sights on a more subtle target, yet one with similarly far-reaching implications. In the name of creating a "colorblind" society, a cadre of policy-makers and activists is seeking to ban the collection of racial demographic information and data on ethnic inequality—the very tools necessary to identify discrimination and to fashion ways of addressing it.

Consider some recent examples:

• In response to California's Proposition 209, which banned state and municipal affirmative action programs, San Diego County refused to collect and report the racial demographics of its public work force. Along similar lines, former Governor Pete Wilson ordered state agencies across California to stop maintaining statistical data on minority and female participation in state contracting, and subsequently vetoed state legislation that would have restored that record-keeping.

• Although it passed by a voice vote in the House, the Senate Judiciary Committee killed the Traffic Stops Statistics Study Act, which would have authorized the collection of data on the race and other characteristics of motorists stopped by police officers. Introduced by Representative John Conyers and supported by the Justice Department, that legislation would have investigated the phenomenon of police stops for "DWB"—Driving While Black or Brown. The act was squelched after the Fraternal Order of Police opposed it on the grounds that it was unnecessary and would have imposed bureaucratic burdens on police. Governor Wilson vetoed similar legislation passed by the California legislature, saying it would demand time, money and human resources while providing "no certain or useful conclusion.". . .

• The strategy of employing "testers"—similarly qualified mock applicants of different races who apply for the same job, apartment or other opportunity in order to determine whether discrimination is afoot—has been endorsed by the Supreme Court and used in the fair-housing context for three decades. Yet in 1998 the House GOP leaders assailed the Equal Employment Opportunity Commission (EEOC) for employing the tactic to detect job discrimination. Republicans threatened to withhold funds needed to clear the backlog of cases at the EEOC unless the commission dropped its plans for expanded testing, which it did.

Opposing Civil Rights

The assault on racial data collection has been led by opponents of civil rights enforcement and couched in the rhetoric of "color-blindness" and dismantling bureaucracy that has characterized anti-affirmative action campaigns. James Glassman of the American Enterprise Institute (AEI), for example, complains that "the tyranny of government racial policies forces us to define ourselves as white, black, Hispanic or Asian. The purpose may be benign (to track the progress of minorities) but the effect is vicious (to reinforce strict racial identity, the way segregationists did)." Dinesh D'Souza, also of AEI, argues in a 1996 *National Review* article that government agencies should not "embrace racial categorization." In the same article he endorses the policy of "allowing private actors to be free to discriminate as they wish."

Whatever one's view of affirmative action, racial don't ask, don't tell rules are bad public policy that frustrates principles and values that enjoy broad public support. First, reliable racial data are crucial to enforcing our basic laws against intentional racial discrimination, which enjoy broad public support. For example, in order to demonstrate that an employer is engaging in a broad-based "pattern or practice" of discrimination in violation of the Civil Rights Act of 1964, a plaintiff must rely on statistical proof that goes beyond the plight of an individual employee. Supreme Court precedent in such cases requires plaintiffs to show a statistically significant disparity between the proportion of qualified minorities in the local labor market and the proportion within the employer's work force. A disparity of more than two standard deviations creates a legal presumption that intentional discrimination is occurring, since a disparity of that magnitude almost never occurs by accident.

The Need for Reliable Racial Data

Demographic information, in other words, provides the "big picture" that places individual incidents in context. Voting rights cases require similar proof, as do many housing discrimination cases and suits challenging the discriminatory use of federal funds. Without reliable racial statistics, it would be virtually impossible for courts or agencies to detect institutional bias, and antidiscrimination laws would go unenforced. More fundamentally, we simply cannot know as a society how far we've come in conquering racial discrimination and inequality without accurate information about the health, progress and opportunities available to communities of different races.

In response to President Bill Clinton's national conversation on race, for example, 1998's Economic Report of the President—an annual review of economic trends produced by the Council of Economic Advisors (CEA)—included for the first time a chapter analyzing income inequality among racial and ethnic groups. The report concluded, among other things, that the significant decrease in the black/white income gap, which occurred in the decade after 1965, virtually halted in 1975, with no meaningful improvement since that time. As economist Glenn Loury noted in the April 6, 1998, *New Republic*, "the clear implication of the CEA report is that, even today, inequality between the races is a problem worthy of national attention."

Behind such statistics lie stark human consequences. Take the case of my Harvard Law School classmate Robert Wilkins. A distinguished attorney at Washington, DC's Public Defender Service, Wilkins was stopped by a Maryland state trooper on I-95 while returning with relatives from his grandfather's funeral in 1992. When Wilkins, an African-American, refused to consent to a search of his rental car—as was his constitutional right—the trooper called in a K-9 unit to search the car over Wilkins's objection. Wilkins and his family endured the indignity and discomfort of standing in the rain during the forty-five-minute search as passing drivers looked on. At the conclusion of the search—which produced no evidence of wrongdoing—Wilkins received a speeding ticket. Wilkins sued under the

Constitution and, as part of a favorable settlement, required the Maryland State Police to record the race of motorists they detain in traffic stops.

Although troopers knew that their activities were being monitored, the results were staggering: While nearly 74 percent of drivers on the Maryland I-95 corridor are white and 17 percent black, more than 72 percent of those stopped and searched by police are black. Every single one of the motorists stopped by one officer during the measured period was an African-American. Because blacks and whites were found to be carrying drugs in roughly the same proportions, discriminatory stops resulted in far more arrests of black motorists than of white ones. Similar patterns have been reported in New Jersey, where, in 1998, troopers shot and wounded three unarmed men—three African-Americans and one Latino—after stopping their van on the New Jersey Turnpike. After an investigation of state police patrol patterns, the New Jersey attorney general issued a report conceding that "minority motorists have been treated differently than non-minority motorists during the course of traffic stops on the New Jersey Turnpike." The report went on to conclude that "the problem of disparate treatment is real—not imagined." That investigation, too, required reliable racial statistics.

Uncovering Racial Bias

Evidence of the importance of racial data collection abounds in virtually every social arena. Recently, analysis of arson and hate-crime data helped to identify a rash of church burnings targeted primarily at African-American congregations. According to the federal Community Relations Service, more than 500 churches in thirteen Southern states were burned or desecrated during 1996 and 1997. Once the dimensions of the problem were identified, focused efforts by government, community groups and others stemmed the attacks and brought a spate of convictions. . . .

Along with data collection, techniques such as "discrimination testing" to investigate alleged racial bias have also proven crucial. Such testing by social scientists and law enforcement over the past decade has provided powerful evidence that discrimination against people of color persists in a range of housing and employment markets, consumer and business transactions, and other contexts. Studies conducted in five different housing markets, for example, found that real estate agents discriminated against Latino and African-American home seekers 40 percent to 50 percent of the time in terms of information offered, efforts to complete transactions, assistance provided regarding financing and credit checks or steering of applicants toward certain neighborhoods.

Racial Considerations on the Census

The politics of race and ethnic heritage have changed greatly over the years, and the census questions [on ethnicity] and their ramifications have changed with it, states Melissa Nobles, a political science professor at the Massachusetts Institute of Technology. The civil-rights movement of the 1960s brought new attention to race data, and states began to use racial information when drawing legislative districts, says Dr. Nobles.

Census data on race—once a treasure trove for slavery advocates and segregationists—began to be used for purposes that would help minorities, including affirmative action and federal aid programs.

Rick Klein, *Dallas Morning News*, March 26, 2000.

Using a similar approach, researchers at Georgetown University discovered bias in a surprising form. The GU study, released in January 1999, asked 720 primary-care physicians how they would manage simulated patients. Black and white actors of both sexes portrayed the patients, who described identical symptoms, risk factors and other relevant information. Yet the physicians said they would refer blacks and women to heart specialists for cardiac catheterization tests only 60 percent as often as they would prescribe the procedure for white male patients. Whether that disparity springs from intentional bias or subconscious perceptions and stereotypes, it has devastating consequences. As US Surgeon General David Satcher noted in response to the study, "It's a matter of life and death whether a patient gets cardiac catheterization with a follow-up of a coronary artery bypass or another therapy. . . .

Blacks are 40 percent more likely [than whites] to die from heart disease, and this could be one factor."

Enforced Ignorance

Given the power of reliable racial information, one must wonder whether policies banning racial data collection are, at bottom, simply an attempt to win the public debate about racial justice and equal opportunity through enforced ignorance. The erosion of public support for civil rights policies in the past decade corresponds to opinion research showing that a large majority of whites now believe that racial discrimination is no longer a significant impediment for people of color. In one study, approximately 75 percent of whites surveyed denied that blacks face discriminatory obstacles in acquiring jobs or housing. People of all races who do not believe that discrimination exists are unlikely to support meaningful civil rights enforcement. Understanding that dynamic, anti-civil rights think tanks have flooded the marketplace with books contending that discrimination has simply ceased. Selling this message is exponentially easier when reliable information to refute it is not available.

Addressing Concerns About Racial Statistics

To the extent that racial data gathering and investigation raise legitimate concerns, those concerns may be addressed through means far less drastic than abolition. Given the many ugly ways in which ethnicity has historically been used in our country, racial questions can raise suspicions and discomfort among people of all races. In light of documented discrimination against African-Americans by the Farmers Home Administration, for example, a black farmer might reasonably hesitate to provide her racial identity to the agency. More broadly, people of all ethnicities who correctly believe that race is a morally irrelevant and artificial characteristic may not understand how racial identity could be a pertinent subject of inquiry.

The way to address these issues is not through denial or suppression but through transparency. People have a right to know how their personal information will be used, and that is particularly true of racial information. Outside of those contexts where the relevance of race is plain—such as physical descriptions of suspects or identification documents such as driver's licenses—explanations of purpose may be necessary to allay suspicion and discomfort.

Concerns about bureaucracy and paperwork also have some legitimacy. Excessive administrative burdens can slow the operation of government and, in extreme cases, may deter officials from performing their duties. But that is true of all paperwork, not just the collection of racial data, and it must be balanced against the government's public mission. The central function of government agencies is to enforce and implement the law. That law includes the equal protection clause of the Constitution and civil rights statutes. Policy-makers should thus consider the problem of reducing paperwork holistically, rather than allowing that problem to subvert civil rights principles.

The same may be said of testing for discrimination, which some oppose as burdensome and deceptive to businesses being investigated. That rationale is tantamount to banning undercover investigations into government corruption, healthcare fraud or drug trafficking on the grounds that such investigations mislead unsuspecting employees and may disrupt or waste the time of legitimate businesses. The answer in each case is that those side effects can be minimized by careful preliminary investigation and, in any event, are easily outweighed by the importance of exposing harmful, illegal conduct.

Finally, it bears noting that facts belong to no one group or agenda, to no ideology or political party. Racial statistics are used not only by civil rights advocates but also by social scientists, policy-makers and such conservative writers as Stephan and Abigail Thernstrom, who continue to argue that racism and discrimination are no longer significant problems in our country. And that is as it should be. Information and the liberty to use it in public discourse are hallmarks of a free society. Efforts to suppress information gathering are threats not merely to the political left or right, but to the truth.

> *"Neither racial pride nor racial kinship offers guidance that is intellectually, morally, or politically satisfactory."*

Racial Pride Is Counterproductive

Randall Kennedy

Many racial and ethnic minorities express pride in their culture and claim that they feel more loyal toward members of their own race than with others. In the following viewpoint, Harvard Law School professor Randall Kennedy contests this view of racial pride. Kennedy maintains that one's individual qualities and accomplishments—not one's skin color or physical features—should be the object of pride. Kennedy, who is black, writes that he feels a kinship with all those who have fought for racial justice. However, he does not believe that he should limit this gratitude to other courageous blacks, since many whites also participated in the civil rights struggle. He argues that loyalties and affiliations should be based on deeds, not inherited features.

As you read, consider the following questions:

1. How does Kennedy describe political theorist Michael Sandel's concept of "the unencumbered self"?
2. What examples does the author use to debunk the notion that "a race *is* a family"?
3. What negative effects can racial pride have on intraracial relations, in Kennedy's opinion?

Excerpted from "My Race Problem—and Ours," by Randall Kennedy, *The Atlantic Monthly*, May 1997. Reprinted with permission from the author.

What is the proper role of race in determining how I, an American black, should feel toward others? One response is that although I should not dislike people because of their race, there is nothing wrong with having a special—a *racial*—affection for other black people. Indeed, many would go further and maintain that something would be wrong with me if I did not sense and express racial pride, racial kinship, racial patriotism, racial loyalty, racial solidarity—synonyms for that amalgam of belief, intuition, and commitment that manifests itself when blacks treat blacks with more solicitude than they do those who are not black.

Some conduct animated by these sentiments has blended into the background of daily routine, as when blacks who are strangers nonetheless speak to each other—"Hello," "Hey," "Yo"—or hug or give each other a soul handshake or refer to each other as "brother" or "sister." Other manifestations are more dramatic. For example, the Million Man March, which brought at least 500,000 black men to Washington, D.C., in 1995, was a demonstration predicated on the notion that blackness gives rise to racial obligation and that black people should have a special, closer, more affectionate relationship with their fellow blacks than with others in America's diverse society.

I reject this response to the question. Neither racial pride nor racial kinship offers guidance that is intellectually, morally, or politically satisfactory.

Racial Pride

I eschew racial pride because of my conception of what should properly be the object of pride for an individual: something that he or she has accomplished. I can feel pride in a good deed I have done or a good effort I have made. I cannot feel pride in some state of affairs that is independent of my contribution to it. The color of my skin, the width of my nose, the texture of my hair, and the various other signs that prompt people to label me black constitute such a state of affairs. I did not achieve my racial designation. It was something I inherited—like my nationality and socio-economic starting place and sex—and therefore something I should not feel proud of or be credited with. In taking this position I follow Frederick Douglass, the great nineteenth-century reformer, who declared that "the only excuse for pride in individuals . . . is in the fact of their own achievements." If the sun has created curled hair and tanned skin, Douglass observed, "let the sun be proud of its achievement."

It is understandable why people have often made inherited group status an honorific credential. Personal achievement is difficult to attain, and the lack of it often leaves a vacuum that racial pride can easily fill. Thus even if a person has little to show for himself, racial pride gives him status.

But maybe I am misconstruing what people mean by racial pride; perhaps it means simply that one is unashamed of one's race. To that I have no objection. No one should be ashamed of the labeling by which she or he is racially categorized, because no one chooses her or his parents or the signs by which society describes and sorts people. For this very same reason, however, no one should congratulate herself on her race insofar as it is merely an accident of birth.

I suspect, however, that when most black people embrace the term "racial pride," they mean more than that they are unembarrassed by their race. They mean, echoing Marcus Garvey, that "to be [black] is no disgrace, but an honor." Thus when James Brown sings "Say It Loud—I'm Black and I'm Proud," he is heard by many blacks as expressing not just the absence of shame but delight and assertiveness in valuing a racial designation that has long been stigmatized in America.

There is an important virtue in this assertion of the value of black life. It combats something still eminently in need of challenge: the assumption that because of their race black people are stupid, ugly, and low, and that because of their race white people are smart, beautiful, and righteous. But within some of the forms that this assertiveness has taken are important vices—including the belief that because of racial kinship blacks ought to value blacks more highly than others.

Racial Kinship

I reject the notion of racial kinship. I do so in order to avoid its burdens and to be free to claim what the distinguished political theorist Michael Sandel labels "the unencumbered self." The unencumbered self is free and independent, "un-

48

encumbered by aims and attachments it does not choose for itself," Sandel writes. "Freed from the sanctions of custom and tradition and inherited status, unbound by moral ties antecedent to choice, the self is installed as sovereign, cast as the author of the only obligations that constrain." Sandel believes that the unencumbered self is an illusion and that the yearning for it is a manifestation of a shallow liberalism that "cannot account for certain moral and political obligations that we commonly recognize, even prize"—"obligations of solidarity, religious duties, and other moral ties that may claim us for reasons unrelated to a choice," which are "indispensable aspects of our moral and political experience." Sandel's objection to those who, like me, seek the unencumbered self is that they fail to appreciate loyalties and responsibilities that should be accorded moral force partly because they influence our identity, such that living by these attachments "is inseparable from understanding ourselves as the particular persons we are—as members of this family or city or nation or people, as bearers of that history, as citizens of this republic."

I admire Sandel's work and have learned much from it. But a major weakness in it is a conflation of "is" and "ought." Sandel privileges what exists and has existed so much that his deference to tradition lapses into historical determinism. He faults the model of the unencumbered self because, he says, it cannot account for feelings of solidarity and loyalty that most people have not chosen to impose upon themselves but that they cherish nonetheless. This represents a fault, however, only if we believe that the unchosen attachments Sandel celebrates should be accorded moral weight. I am not prepared to do that simply on the basis that such attachments exist, have long existed, and are passionately felt. Feelings of primordial attachment often represent mere prejudice or superstition, a hangover of the childhood socialization from which many people never recover.

A Race Is Not a Family

One defense of racial kinship takes the shape of an analogy between race and family. This position was strikingly advanced by the nineteenth-century black-nationalist intellectual Alexander Crummell, who asserted that "a race *is* a family," that "race feeling, like the family feeling, is of divine origin," and that the extinction of race feeling is thus—fortunately, in his view—just as impossible as the extinction of family feeling.

Analogizing race to family is a potent rhetorical move used to challenge those who, like me, are animated by a liberal, individualistic, and universalistic ethos that is skeptical of, if not hostile to, the particularisms—national, ethnic, religious, and racial—that seem to have grown so strong recently, even in arenas, such as major cosmopolitan universities, where one might have expected their demise. The central point of the challenge is to suggest that the norms I embrace will, or at least should, wobble and collapse in the face of claims on familial loyalty. Blood, as they say, is thicker than water.

Whites and Racial Justice

[In the 1960s] there were some white people who went to the back of the bus, and sat and were arrested or ejected because they wouldn't move from the back of the bus. Who were these people, what were they about, what movements were they a part of? . . .

It's too complicated to reduce to "white people are bad and black people are good."

Robin Kelley, quoted in *Witness*, April 1997.

One way to deal with the race-family analogy is to question its aptness on the grounds that a race is so much more populous than what is commonly thought of as a family that race cannot give rise to the same, or even similar, feelings of loyalty. When we think of a family, we think of a small, close-knit association of people who grow to know one another intimately over time. A race, in contrast, is a conglomeration of strangers. Black men at the Million Man March assuredly called one another brothers. But if certain questions were posed ("Would you be willing to lend a hundred dollars to this brother, or donate a kidney to that one?"), it would have quickly become clear that many, if not most, of those "brothers" perceived one another as strangers—not so distant as whites, perhaps, but strangers nonetheless.

However, I do not want to rest my argument here. Rather, I want to accept the race-family analogy in order to strengthen my attack on assumptions that privilege status-driven loyalties (the loyalties of blood) over chosen loyalties (the loyalties of will). In my view, many people, including legislators and judges, make far too much of blood ties in derogation of ties created by loving effort.

A vivid illustration is provided by the following kind of child-custody decision. It involves a child who has been separated from her parents and placed with adults who assume the role of foster parents. These adults nurture her, come to love her, and ultimately seek legally to become her new parents. If the "blood" parents of the child do not interfere, the foster parents will have a good chance of doing this. If, however, the blood parents say they want "their" child back, authorities in many jurisdictions will privilege the blood connection and return the child—even if the initial separation is mainly attributable to the fault of the blood parents, even if the child has been with the foster parents for a long time and is prospering under their care, even if the child views the foster parents as her parents and wants to stay with them, and even if there is good reason to believe that the foster parents will provide a more secure home setting than the child's blood parents. Judges make such rulings in large part because they reflect the idolatry of "blood," which is an ideological cousin to the racial beliefs I oppose.

Am I saying that, morally, blood ties are an insufficient, indeed bad, basis for preferring one's genetic relatives to others? Yes. I will rightly give the only life jacket on the sinking ship to my mother as opposed to your mother, because I love my mother (or at least I love her more than yours). I love my mother, however, not because of a genetic tie but because over time she has done countless things that make me want to love her. She took care of me when I could not take care of myself. She encouraged me. She provided for my future by taking me to the doctor when appropriate, disciplining me, giving me advice, paying for my education. I love her, too, because of qualities I have seen her exhibit in interactions with others—my father, my brother, my sister, neighbors, colleagues, adversaries. The biological connection helped to create the framework in which I have been able to see and experience her lovable qualities. But it is deeds, not blood—doing, not being—that is the morally appropriate basis for my preference for my mother over all other mothers in the world.

Solidarity with Whites

Some contend, though, that "doing" is what lies at the foundation of black racial kinship—that the reason one should feel morally compelled by virtue of one's blackness to have and show racial solidarity toward other blacks is that preceding generations of black people did things animated by racial loyalty which now benefit all black people. These advocates would contend that the benefits bestowed—for instance, *Brown v. Board of Education*, the Civil Rights Act of 1964, the Voting Rights Act of 1965, and affirmative-action programs—impose upon blacks correlative racial obligations. That is what many are getting at when they say that all blacks, but particularly affluent ones, have a racial obligation to "give back" to the black community.

I agree that one should be grateful to those who have waged struggles for racial justice, sometimes at tremendous sacrifice. But why should my gratitude be racially bounded? Elijah Lovejoy, a white man murdered in Alton, Illinois, in 1837 for advocating the abolition of slavery, participated just as fervently in that great crusade as any person of my hue. The same could be said of scores of other white abolitionists. Coming closer to our time, not only courageous black people, such as Medgar Evers, Vernon Dahmer, and James Chaney, fought white supremacy in the shadow of death during the struggle for civil rights in the Deep South. White people like James Reeb and Viola Liuzzo were there too, as were Andrew Goodman and Michael Schwerner. Against this history I see no reason why paying homage to the struggle for racial justice and endeavoring to continue that struggle must entail any sort of racially stratified loyalty. Indeed, this history suggests the opposite. . . .

It is noteworthy that those who have most ostentatiously

asserted the imperatives of black racial solidarity—I think here particularly of Marcus Garvey, Elijah Muhammad, and Louis Farrakhan—are also those who have engaged in the most divisive, destructive, and merciless attacks on "brothers" and "sisters" who wished to follow a different path. My objection to the claims of racial pride and kinship stems in part from my fears of the effect on interracial relations. But it stems also in large part from my fears of the stultifying effect on intraracial relations. Racial pride and kinship seem often to stunt intellectual independence. If racial loyalty is deemed essential and morally virtuous, then a black person's adoption of positions that are deemed racially disloyal will be seen by racial loyalists as a supremely threatening sin, one warranting the harsh punishments that have historically been visited upon alleged traitors.

If one looks at the most admirable efforts by activists to overcome racial oppression in the United States, one finds people who yearn for justice, not merely for the advancement of a particular racial group. One finds people who do not replicate the racial alienations of the larger society but instead welcome interracial intimacy of the most profound sorts. One finds people who are not content to accept the categories of communal affiliation they have inherited but instead insist upon bringing into being new and better forms of communal affiliation, ones in which love and loyalty are unbounded by race. I think here of Wendell Phillips and certain sectors of the abolitionist movement. I also think of James Farmer and the early years of the Congress of Racial Equality, and John Lewis and the early years of the Student Nonviolent Coordinating Committee. My favorite champion of this ethos, however, is a person I quoted at the beginning of this article, a person whom the sociologist Orlando Patterson aptly describes as "undoubtedly the most articulate former slave who ever lived," a person with whose words I would like to end. Frederick Douglass literally bore on his back the stigmata of racial oppression. Speaking in June of 1863, only five months after the Emancipation Proclamation and before the complete abolition of slavery, Douglass gave a talk titled "The Present and Future of the Colored Race in America," in which he asked whether "the white and colored people of this country [can] be blended into a common nationality, and enjoy together . . . under the same flag, the inestimable blessings of life, liberty, and the pursuit of happiness, as neighborly citizens of a common country." He answered: "I believe they can."

I, too, believe we can, if we are willing to reconsider and reconstruct the basis of our feelings of pride and kinship.

"*I embrace racial kinship because it is a necessity for Black survival.*"

Racial Pride Is Beneficial

Paul King

Paul King is the chairman of UBM Incorporated, the largest black-owned construction firm in Chicago, Illinois. In the following viewpoint, King argues that feelings of racial loyalty and kinship have ensured the survival and progress of African Americans. In the United States, he explains, racial identity has the largest influence on an individual's self-concept and personality development; race also signifies culture and community. Those who reject feelings of pride and loyalty toward others of their own racial community suffer from a form of self-hatred, King contends. He points out, for example, that racially disloyal blacks have been known to work against changes that have benefited other blacks.

As you read, consider the following questions:

1. In King's opinion, what is the "double encumbrance" of being black in America?
2. According to the author, how has the development and recruitment of African-American managers benefited employees of other races at UBM Incorporated?
3. Which two contemporary African Americans have committed "the ultimate disloyalty" against black people, in King's opinion?

Reprinted from "A Matter of Pride," by Paul King, *Emerge*, October 1997. Reprinted with permission from the author.

Harvard law professor Randall Kennedy, in the May 1997 issue of *The Atlantic Monthly*, promotes for African-Americans something that Black psychologist Bobby E. Wright, in the 1970s, dubbed mentacide—a cultural suicide, of sorts, a psychological assassination. In this essay, "My Race Problem—And Ours," Kennedy argues that Black people should forsake racial pride in favor of individual achievements:

> I eschew racial pride because of my conception of what should properly be the object of pride for an individual: something that he or she has accomplished. I can feel pride in a good deed I have done or a good effort I have made," he writes. "I cannot feel pride in some state of affairs that is independent of my contribution to it. . . . I did not achieve my racial designation.

I, however, an African-American businessman born and reared in Chicago, reside ideologically in the same neighborhood as Pulitzer prize–winning playwright August Wilson. He states:

> I believe that race matters—that is the largest, most identifiable and most important part of our personality. It is the largest category of identification because it is the one that most influences your perception of yourself, and it is the one to which others in the world of men most respond. Race is also an important part of the American landscape, as America is made up of an amalgamation of races from all parts of the globe. Race is also the product of a shared gene pool that allows for group identification, and it is an organizing principle around which cultures are formed. When I say culture I am speaking about the behavior patterns, arts, beliefs, institutions and all other products of human work and thought as expressed in a particular community of people.

Racially Motivated Pride

I have pride in opera soprano Leontyne Price, who came from Laurel, Miss., at a time when Black people were lynched routinely. Yet she had the persistence, focus, discipline and talent to prevail in a Eurocentric medium in spite of hostile and subtle attempts to stop her.

I have pride in Glenn Harston, a young Black man who wanted to be an iron worker in Chicago in 1967. White union members threatened to push him from a high-rise girder to his death if he tried to integrate their union. Not only did Harston become a tradesman, but he went on to become a successful businessman who recently celebrated his son's college graduation.

I am proud of Harold Washington, who became Chicago's first African-American mayor. He prevailed despite the dismal predications of Whites that the city would collapse, bond ratings would plunge, city services would cease and the quality of city life would tumble if a Black man were elected chief executive.

I am proud of Nelson Mandela, who withstood decades of South Africa's apartheid, imprisonment and emotional torture. He had the strength of will and purpose to emerge victorious against his racist foes.

Nelson Mandela, Harold Washington, Glenn Harston and Leontyne Price succeeded in a climate of racial hostility and animosity that still persists today. Their courage, tenacity and refusal to surrender in spite of White resistance gives me racially motivated pride.

That pride extends to more ordinary accomplishments among African-Americans: to those Black mothers who struggle to obtain their associate degrees in community colleges and to their wayward sons who drop out of school but work hard to earn a general equivalency diploma (GED). To deny the joy of their winning against formidable odds would be the equivalent of me hating myself. That Black people succeed in a hostile environment gives me the moral basis to identify with and take pride in their achievements.

There Is No "Unencumbered Self"

Kennedy rejects such racial kinship in favor of the "unencumbered self." Quoting political theorist Michael Sandel, Kennedy explains:

> The unencumbered self is free and independent, "unencumbered by aims and attachments it does not choose for itself. . . . Freed from the sanctions of custom and tradition and inherited status, unbound by moral ties antecedent to choice, the self is installed as sovereign, cast as the author of the only obligations that constrain."

Sandel, Kennedy writes, believes the unencumbered self is an illusion. So do I. I embrace racial kinship because it is a necessity for Black survival. Unfortunately, being Black in America requires a double encumbrance: an extraordinary effort to achieve and a stubborn balance of mind to navigate the racist minefields that we African-Americans face daily. No one can expect to sail through life without the burdens and responsibilities that society demands.

How Kennedy can oppose racial kinship after having clerked for Supreme Court Justice Thurgood Marshall is beyond me. Marshall was obviously motivated by more than moral outrage in his legal championship of Black causes. Expressing his love and admiration for Southern Black people, he once said:

> There isn't a threat known to men that they do not receive. They're never out from under pressure. I don't think I could take it for a week. The possibility of violent death for them and their families is something they've learned to live with like a man learns to sleep with a sore arm.

It is even more bewildering how Kennedy can invoke Frederick Douglass to support his outlandish ideas. Douglass, a former slave, felt enough kinship with slaves and later Black freedmen to become a race champion and staunch abolitionist.

Kennedy may be ambivalent as to whom he owes for creating the environment in which he has achieved professional and material success. But he—like every other African-American—has his lineage tied to slavery and kinship with those Black people who over the centuries survived, thereby allowing us to carry on this debate today.

Still, for Kennedy, such pride, kinship and loyalty are a burden, and he wonders whether Black people in positions of authority who choose to carry this racial loyalty will be dragged down by it. "Black employers or personnel directors face the question of whether racial loyalties should shape their decisions," he writes.

Opening Closed Doors

Again, I must differ. My company, UBM, is the largest Black-owned construction business in Chicago. The construction industry has been one of the most racially exclusive industries in the United States, and the doors routinely have been closed to African-Americans at every level. In 1969, I led the first shutdown of Chicago construction sites. I confronted Whites—engaged in the worst kind of racial kinship—who said that if they allowed Black people into the union the buildings would fall down. Our shutdowns helped open up many of those closed doors.

Nearly 30 years later, African-Americans are still playing catch-up in this business. For some time, my company has been trying to hire Black project managers and other executives capable of overseeing $2 million or $3 million projects—a normal workload for such construction professionals. Guess what? There are none. The construction industry, with its decades of excluding Black people, has left us with a professional pool absent of African-Americans who have the prerequisite college diplomas or tradesman-level experience—credentials that impart the confidence, initiative and technical competence needed to qualify for project manager positions.

What would Kennedy have had me do? Wring my hands and give up?

The Need for Kinship

I believe that African-Americans currently are under probably the greatest attack since Reconstruction. This may very well be the fourth time the larger society has tried to figure out what to do with us—slavery, Reconstruction, the '60s and now. The absolute revision and destruction of affirmative action; the level of police brutality; the failure of educational institutions: When you look at all of that, it suggests to me that business leaders and educated people have a responsibility to counter this attack. From a historical perspective, what race of people has ever survived without acknowledging kinship?

Paul King, quoted in *Emerge*, October 1997.

Our company decided to take action and to develop our own candidates. My partners and I launched a college summer internship program. We hired a Black expert to help set up development programs. And now with an annual volume of $20 million, UBM has more African-Americans in decision-making professional positions—estimators, superintendents, computer engineers, civil engineers, marketing executives, accounting, safety, project managers—than many of Chicago's 10 largest White-owned construction companies, whose collective volume exceeds $9 billion nationwide.

The Betterment of All

Kennedy would leap to challenge us: How does this special effort to cultivate Black project managers affect other employees?

I have two partners. One is an African-American woman. The other is Asian Indian. Currently, our full-time staff, about 75 people, is a little more than one-third African-American. The others are White, Indian or Asian. The UBM family knows that corporate tenacity, the mutual respect I have within the Black community, as well as the depth of the relationships within the larger Chicago community, lend to the success that provides them with secure employment to sustain their own families and send their children to college. They know we are committed to giving them respect and a fair shake as we pursue these initiatives to help bring along the African-Americans who have been left behind.

Beyond profits, UBM seeks to give value to clients, to provide a means for employees to have a competitively paying and fulfilling career and to improve conditions in the African-American community. Our company, which will celebrate its 25th anniversary in the year 2000, is working on polishing our skills of management. We are perfecting our employee manual; there are merit awards, there are bonuses. There is a salary administration plan underway. There are written procedures and clearer paths for rewards and termination being developed. We are outlining for all staff the avenues for development and achievement. It's all a work in progress. But we are concerned about the well-being and betterment of everyone: Whites, women, Asians, everybody.

There is no conflict in the elimination of Black disparity and the running of a successful and fair business. A non-Black executive recently proudly reported to me that he assembled an all-Black workforce on one complex project that UBM won with the help of a local Black official. Our success proves there does not have to be a conflict if the owners and staff are committed to doing it.

Racial Disloyalty

I must say, however, that I do find one point of agreement with Kennedy: It is true that a Black person who adopts a racially disloyal position may be viewed by some Black people as threatening and deserving of harsh punishment.

At the end of his essay, Kennedy provides insight as to why he is so vexed by such solidarity:

> My objection to the claims of racial pride and kinship stems in part from my fears of the effect on interracial relations. But it stems also in large part from my fears of the stultifying effect on intraracial relations. Racial pride and kinship seem often to stunt intellectual independence. If racial loyalty is deemed essential and morally virtuous, then a Black person's adoption of positions that are deemed racially disloyal will be seen by racial loyalists as a supremely threatening sin, one warranting the harsh punishments that have historically been visited upon alleged traitors.

For most, the adoption of racially disloyal positions have a transitory effect. I hope that Kennedy's weird statements stimulate debate and that through such debate he will reconsider. Unfortunately, the reverse is more likely. Since White-owned media tend to seize on anti-Black views, Kennedy may end up with a throng of converts who do further damage to Black people.

Legal scholar Derrick Bell speaks to this curious phenomenon in his book, *Faces at the Bottom of the Well*:

> Few blacks avoid diminishment of racial standing, most of their statements about racial conditions being diluted and their recommendations of other blacks taken with a grain of salt. The usual exception to this rule is the black person who publicly disparages or criticizes other blacks who are speaking or acting in ways that upset whites. Instantly, such statements are granted 'enhanced standing' even when the speaker has no special expertise or experience in the subject he or she is criticizing.

But whatever the fallout of Kennedy's words, it pales by comparison with the ultimate disloyalty visited upon Black people by two men: Supreme Court Justice Clarence Thomas and Ward Connerly.

Connerly is steadfast in advocating a philosophy anti-thetical to Black advancement in the United States. He helped pass Proposition 209 with his posturing and pronouncements as a board member of the Regents of the University of California. Prop. 209 eliminated minority contracting, minority hiring and the minority university admission programs. Between 1996 and 1997, he helped reduce Black admission at the University of California at Berkeley's law school from 75 to 14. Only one African-American student enrolled in 1997. And in a spillover effect, at the University of Texas law school—formerly a major educator of Black lawyers—enrollment dropped from about 40 African-American students in previous years to only four in 1997.

Thomas has Connerly beat, though. Thomas is a primary beneficiary of affirmative action and racial pride—from his admittance to Yale's law school, to his executive post at the Equal Employment Opportunity Commission. Even his appointment to the Supreme Court was a "Negro thing"—to fill Thurgood Marshall's seat.

Nonetheless, Thomas has taken an anti-Black stance on congressional redistricting and a vehement position against affirmative action. He helped create the climate in which Prop. 209 was passed. [In 1996, Proposition 209 ended affirmative action programs in California.]

Let us hope that Kennedy eschews such a level of activism, and that his career never reaches the judicial bench where he could do more irreparable harm to Black people. Let us hope that he remains in academia, where his ideas may be debated, then simply fade from the public arena.

| *"Racial segregation is inconsistent with civil democracy."*

Racial Segregation Is Harmful

Florence Wagman Roisman

Florence Wagman Roisman is an associate professor at the Indiana University School of Law in Indianapolis. For many years, she was an attorney with the National Housing Law Project. In the following viewpoint, she discusses several of the pitfalls of racial segregation. "Race" has no biological basis, Roisman claims; it is simply a concept that has been used to grant ethnic groups high or low status in society. Therefore, she argues, labeling and separating people on the basis of race is intrinsically unjust. Racial segregation has resulted in the unfair treatment of members of low-status minority groups—and this in turn has led to poverty and an increase in violent crime. The 1960s' ideal of racial integration deserves continuing support, Roisman concludes.

As you read, consider the following questions:
1. In what ways does segregation waste human resources, according to Roisman?
2. According to the Milton S. Eisenhower Foundation, as quoted by the author, what intensifies violent crime?
3. In Roisman's opinion, what was foolish about some of the activism in the 1960s?

Reprinted from "Is Integration Possible? Of Course . . . ," by Florence Wagman Roisman, *Poverty and Race*, January/February 2000. Reprinted with permission from *Poverty and Race*, info@prrac.org.

Is integration possible? Of course. . . . Not only possible, but absolutely essential.

Here are the "top 6" reasons for acknowledging that we cannot do without "racial" integration—and rejecting its opposite, segregation:

1. Racial segregation is inconsistent with civil democracy. The polity to which we aspire is premised on the equal worth of each human being. Putting ourselves or other people into categories based on the color of their skin—or the color of some ancestor's skin—negates that fundamental principle.

2. Racial segregation is intellectually insupportable. As Audrey Smedley writes in *Race in North America: Origin and Evolution of a Worldview:* "Biological anthropologists, geneticists, and human biologists . . . no longer accept 'race' as having any validity in the biological sciences." The concept of "race" was "fabricated out of social and political realities" to impose "on conquered and enslaved peoples an identity as the lowest status groups in society." As we reject the goals of conquest and enslavement, we must reject also the tool by which they were achieved—the construction of "racial" identity.

3. Racial segregation is silly. It is ludicrous to consider that one knows anything about another human being when all one knows is the color of someone's skin—or the color of the skin of an ancestor of that person. As Benjamin Franklin wrote in *A Narrative of the Late Massacres,* protesting the wholesale killing of friendly Indians: "[S]hould any Man, with a freckled Face and red Hair, kill a Wife or Child of mine, [would] it . . . be right for me to revenge it, by killing all the freckled red-haired Men, Women and Children, I could afterwards anywhere meet with[?]"

Segregation Is Wasteful and Dangerous

4. Racial segregation is wasteful of human resources. One consequence of racial segregation is that the people who are considered "inferior" are confined to particular geographic areas, where schools, jobs, transportation, recreation, public facilities and other opportunities are degraded. Among those who are so confined, and so deprived of opportunities to develop their full human potential, are people who could discover cures for cancer, compose great symphonies, develop

computers that do not crash, and make manifold other immense contributions to human good. By cheating people of those opportunities, we cheat ourselves of what those opportunities could produce.

5. Racial segregation is wasteful of other natural resources. Racial prejudice is a principal cause of the abandonment of the cities and the push ever outward to the suburbs and beyond. And the race-driven "urban sprawl" imposes immense costs in new highway development, with its destruction of farmland, dangers to biodiversity, increased air pollution (exacerbating respiratory illness and promoting climactic change) and social costs.

Gary Markstein. Reprinted with permission from Copley News Service.

6. Racial segregation is dangerous. The likelihood is that dreams deferred will not, in Langston Hughes' words, "dry up like . . . raisin[s] in the sun." They will explode. The riots of past years will seem tame compared to any of the new millennium. As the Milton S. Eisenhower Foundation recently reminded us, the number of firearms in the United States "has just doubled to nearly 200 million—many of them high-powered, easily concealed models 'with no other logi-

cal function than to kill humans.'" The Foundation's report notes that violent crime is exacerbated by a "vast and shameful inequality in income, wealth and opportunity. . . ."

The Mandate of the 21st Century

We have no basis for concluding that integration is not possible . . . but it is difficult and time-consuming. . . .

The racial and ethnic stereotypes—and the notion of white supremacy—that divide us from one another were created over a long period of time and have been buttressed by powerful societal forces. We did not begin seriously to undermine those societal forces and to root out the stereotypes until the 1960's, and our efforts have been sporadic since then. We've relied on under-funded, inconsistent programs and volunteer efforts to turn around a massive propaganda machine that serves potent institutions.

The foolish thing that many of us did in the 60's was to think that the problems of racism and poverty would be solved in that decade. Many of us now recognize that they may not be solved in our lifetimes. But—for all the inadequacy of the remedies—considerable progress has been made, and more will be made if we determine to do it.

Howard Zinn, interviewed by Susan Stamberg on National Public Radio in December 1999, said that the idea of the 20th century that will last into the 21st is "the idea of non-violent direct action"—"precisely because it's been such a century of violence." In the same spirit, I maintain that the 20th century has demonstrated that racial separation is unacceptable: racial integration is the mandate of the 21st century.

8

"As for the supposed main purposes of integration, aiding the education of black students and promoting the closer social harmony of the races, integration simply failed."

Enforced Racial Integration Is Harmful

Samuel Francis

Integration—particularly school integration—is a failed social policy, columnist Samuel Francis argues in the following viewpoint. The Supreme Court decision to desegregate public schools in 1954 led to the busing of students to schools outside of their own neighborhoods. Although it was intended to foster racial harmony and to improve education for black children, Francis writes, mandatory integration only created more racial polarization as whites moved to the suburbs to avoid the influx of blacks to formerly white city schools. Many blacks, moreover, feel insulted by the notion that their children need to go to school with whites in order to succeed. Francis maintains that each race should be allowed to pursue its own self-defined goals.

As you read, consider the following questions:

1. According to Francis, did black student performance improve after school desegregation?
2. In what way is integration "racist," according to the author?
3. In the author's opinion, why did the early civil rights movement suppress racial consciousness?

Someday the Potomac will freeze over in the middle of July and the National Association for the Advancement of Colored People will abandon its support for school integration. The Potomac is still flowing, but with the *New York Times* reporting in 1997 that the NAACP is considering changing its position on integration, there's always hope.

Ever since its founding early in the twentieth century, the NAACP has pushed school integration as virtually the centerpiece of its agenda. Thurgood Marshall, when he was the head of the organization's legal department, argued the case for desegregation before the Supreme Court; civil rights workers crusaded for it; and for decades, all the devices of social and racial engineering—from dubious court decisions to forced busing to federal marshals escorting black students to segregated schools—have been devoted to that goal.

Nevertheless, at its national convention, the NAACP plans to debate whether the goal is worth pursuing. The major names in the organization—its chairwoman, Myrlie Evers-Williams, and Julian Bond, among others—still favor keeping integration on the group's political table, but others have rethought the matter and decided it's time to give it up.

The NAACP giving up on integration is thus a bit like the American Civil Liberties Union deciding that *Playboy* ought to be banned, but all silly things come to an end eventually, and if the group does decide to shelve a decades-old policy that has accomplished almost nothing for anyone, it deserves a round of applause.

The Failure of Integration

Desegregation of public schools, ordered by the Supreme Court in its 1954 *Brown v. Board of Education* decision, is now widely recognized as having been ideologically motivated, dishonestly decided and constitutionally illiterate. Forced busing of school children merely alienated white parents and contributed to racial conflicts. As for the supposed main purposes of integration, aiding the education of black students and promoting the closer social harmony of the races, integration simply failed.

Indeed, forced integration helped promote white flight from the major cities. The influx of black students into previously white schools merely instigated the quiet but rapid migration of middle class whites to the suburbs, and improved performance of black students after integration has been negligible.

Busing Increased Racial Isolation

When Judge W. Arthur Garrity's order first set the buses rolling in Boston, 85,000 students of all races attended the city's public schools. A decade later, enrollment had shrunk to 60,000. "White flight" had begun even before the judge usurped control of the schools, but busing accelerated it sharply. In 1970, there were 62,000 white children in Boston's schools—64 percent of the total. By 1980, the number had dropped to 24,000, a little more than 35 percent of the total. By 1990, the white headcount was down to 13,500, or 22 percent. Today whites account for just 17 percent of Boston's public school students, and most of them attend one of the three exam schools, where admission is based partly on merit.

In short, busing didn't end segregation—it worsened it. The whole purpose of uprooting kids from schools close to home and sending them on long bus rides to neighborhoods they didn't know was to increase interracial exposure. That was precisely the outcome Garrity's orders sabotaged. Before busing began, the average black child in Boston attended a school that was 24 percent white. Now the proportion is 17 percent. All that anguish, all that upheaval—and the schools are more racially isolated than ever.

Jeff Jacoby, *Conservative Chronicle*, January 20, 1999.

A recent study conducted by Harvard University reports that school segregation today remains somewhat higher than before integration was tried. In short, the policy has accomplished nothing except to increase racial polarization to the degree that the president of the United States feels the need to exhort us all to "racial reconciliation."

The Influence of Racial Pride

The critics of integration within the NAACP seem to be moved by these considerations, but they also offer another, that the basic assumption of racial integration is that black students cannot do well unless they are around white students. Hence, integration, a measure largely designed by white liberals, is at least as "racist" as the assumption that blacks don't deserve good education anyway. In what is surely one of the most ironic comments of the year, a black critic of integration, Amos Quick of Greensboro, N.C., writes, "Separate but truly equal would not be so bad."

What lies behind the dissidence in the NAACP, then, is not only recognition that racial integration has been a flop but also the emergence in the last generation or so of an explicitly racial black consciousness that was absent or cleverly kept hidden in an earlier era. To a large degree, the black dissidents don't like the concept of integration with whites because it insults their racial consciousness and the "racial pride" that derives from it.

Consciousness of race was hidden during the earlier stage of the civil rights movement because the movement was predicated on the widely shared assumption that race doesn't really exist or isn't really important. But both white resistance to integration as well as the emergence of black consciousness, as well as the headlines in any newspaper on any given day, prove that it is important. And, if racial consciousness doesn't start arming itself with the power of the state, there's no particular reason to believe that any harm will come of it.

It remains to be seen whether the NAACP will have the guts to cut bait on a legal and social policy that made some of its pioneers famous and powerful but at the expense of the real interests of both races and the country they live in. If its members really do have the courage and the smarts to chuck out a failed and ill-considered policy and let each race seek its own goals without the federal leviathan at its back, the races might actually find that they get along with each other better than they did in the age of racial denial from which the ideal of integration sprang.

Periodical Bibliography

The following articles have been selected to supplement the diverse views presented in this chapter. Addresses are provided for periodicals not indexed in the *Readers' Guide to Periodical Literature*, the *Alternative Press Index*, the *Social Sciences Index*, or the *Index to Legal Periodicals and Books*.

Natalie Angier	"Do Races Differ? Not Really, Genes Show," *New York Times*, August 22, 2000.
Amitai Etzioni	"Some Diversity," *Society*, July 1998.
Roy Innis and Niger Innis	"Ending Race-Based Politics," *American Outlook*, Summer 2000. Available from the Hudson Institute, 5395 Emerson Way, Indianapolis, IN 46226.
Margo Jefferson	"The Presence of Race in Politically Correct Ambiguity," *New York Times*, February 8, 1999.
John Lewis	"Forgiving George Wallace," *New York Times*, September 16, 1998.
Tom Montgomery-Fate	"Beyond the Multiculture," *The Other Side*, March/April 1997. Available from 300 W. Apsley St., Philadelphia, PA 19144.
New York Times Magazine	"How Race Is Lived in America: A Special Issue in Pictures, Dialogue, and Memoir," July 16, 2000.
Orlando Patterson	"The Race Trap," *New York Times*, July 11, 1997.
Valerie Richardson	"Myth of Multiculturalism?" *Insight*, October 19, 1998. Available from 3600 New York Ave. NE, Washington, DC 20002.
Beverly Daniel Tatum	"Overcoming the Culture of Silence on Race . . . ," *Christian Science Monitor*, September 2, 1997.
Ann Scott Tyson	"Black Support Wanes for Goal of Integration," *Christian Science Monitor*, July 17, 1997.
G. Pascal Zachary	"A Mixed Future," *Wall Street Journal*, January 1, 2000.

CHAPTER 2

Will Immigration Lead to an Interracial Crisis?

Chapter Preface

Demographic research suggests that by 2050, America's Asian, Hispanic, black, and mixed-race populations will have increased while the white population will have decreased. The percentage of Latinos, for example, will increase from 10.2 percent to 24.5 percent, and the Asian population will increase from 3.3 percent to 8.2 percent. In the meantime, the percentage of whites in the population will decrease from 74 percent to 53 percent, while the black population will remain fairly stable, rising from 12 percent to 13.6 percent.

Some analysts worry that higher birthrates among Asian and Hispanic Americans, along with an increase in immigration from Asia and Latin America, is a threat to national unity. They fear that America could become gripped by dangerous racial and socioeconomic conflicts as competing ethnic groups fight to promote their interests at the expense of all others. If this happens, these analysts maintain, the United States will become a fragmented nation—a young democracy thwarted by barriers of language, culture, and race. As journalist Jared Taylor warns, "Diversity of race or tribe or language or religion are the main reasons people are at each other's throats all around the world. Just pick up a newspaper. Diversity . . . is strife, not strength."

Others express optimism about the upcoming population changes, noting that the United States has always been a nation of immigrants. These optimists have hopes that Americans will welcome the country's increasing diversity and build communities based on shared values, economic justice, and respect for differences. If this comes to pass, they argue, the United States will persevere as the world's first truly multiracial democracy. In a 1997 speech, Bill Clinton expressed confidence about a future rich in cultural variety: "The diverse backgrounds and talents of our citizens can help America to light the globe, showing nations deeply divided by race, religion and tribe that there is a better way."

The authors in the following chapter present further debate about the implications of America's changing racial and ethnic demographics.

"*[It is] possible . . . that the nation will
continue to fracture into many separate,
disconnected communities with no shared
sense of commonality or purpose.*"

Immigration Threatens
America's Unity

William Booth

In the following viewpoint, *Washington Post* staff writer
William Booth discusses the implications of America's
changing racial and ethnic demographics. The recent wave
of Hispanic and Asian immigrants is raising concerns about
the future of American national identity, he points out.
While the U.S. population is becoming more diverse, a disturbing amount of ethnic segregation and racial discord persists. Tensions increase as native-born Americans and immigrants compete for jobs, neighborhoods, and political power,
maintains Booth. Many immigrants, furthermore, cling to
their ethnic heritage and resist identifying themselves as
American. In the end, some experts claim, massive immigration could create a nation that is sharply divided by regional,
economic, and cultural differences.

As you read, consider the following questions:
1. According to Booth, when did the United States
   experience its largest wave of immigration?
2. According to the U.S. Census Bureau, Hispanics will
   comprise what percent of the American population by
   the year 2050?
3. What is the nature of today's "white flight," according to
   the author?

At the beginning of the twentieth century, as steamers poured into American ports, their steerages filled with European immigrants, a Jew from England named Israel Zangwill penned a play whose story line has long been forgotten, but whose central theme has not. His production was entitled *"The Melting Pot"* and its message still holds a tremendous power on the national imagination—the promise that all immigrants can be transformed into Americans, a new alloy forged in a crucible of democracy, freedom and civic responsibility.

In 1908, when the play opened in Washington, D.C., the United States was in the middle of absorbing the largest influx of immigrants in its history—Irish and Germans, followed by Italians and East Europeans, Catholics and Jews—some 18 million new citizens between 1890 and 1920.

Today, the United States is experiencing its second great wave of immigration, a movement of people that has profound implications for a society that by tradition pays homage to its immigrant roots at the same time it confronts complex and deeply ingrained ethnic and racial divisions.

The immigrants of today come not from Europe but overwhelmingly from the still developing world of Asia and Latin America. They are driving a demographic shift so rapid that within the lifetimes of today's teenagers, no one ethnic group—including whites of European descent—will comprise a majority of the nation's population.

This shift, according to social historians, demographers and others studying the trends, will severely test the premise of the fabled melting pot, the idea, so central to national identity, that this country can transform people of every color and background into "one America."

Just as possible, they say, is that the nation will continue to fracture into many separate, disconnected communities with no shared sense of commonality or purpose. Or perhaps it will evolve into something in between, a pluralistic society that will hold on to some core ideas about citizenship and capitalism, but with little meaningful interaction among groups.

The demographic changes raise other questions about political and economic power. Will that power, now held disproportionately by whites, be shared in the new America? What will happen when Hispanics overtake blacks as the nation's single largest minority?

"I do not think that most Americans really understand the historic changes happening before their very eyes," says Peter Salins, an immigration scholar who is provost of the State Universities of New York. "What are we going to become? Who are we? How do the newcomers fit in—and how do the natives handle it—this is the great unknown."

An Emphasis on Ethnicity

Fear of strangers, of course, is nothing new in American history. The last great immigration wave produced a bitter backlash, epitomized by the Chinese Exclusion Act of 1882 and the return, in the 1920s, of the Ku Klux Klan, which not only targeted blacks but Catholics, Jews and immigrants as well.

But despite this strife, many historians argue that there was a greater consensus in the past on what it meant to be an American, a yearning for a common language and culture, and a desire—encouraged, if not coerced by members of the dominant white Protestant culture—to assimilate. Today, they say, there is more emphasis on preserving one's ethnic identity, of finding ways to highlight and defend one's cultural roots.

More often than not, the neighborhoods where Americans live, the politicians and propositions they vote for, the cultures they immerse themselves in, the friends and spouses they have, the churches and schools they attend, and the way they view themselves are defined by ethnicity. The question is whether, in the midst of such change, there is also enough glue to hold Americans together.

"As we become more and more diverse, there is all this potential to make that reality work for us," says Angela Oh, a Korean American activist who emerged as a powerful voice for Asian immigrants after the Los Angeles riots in 1992. "But yet, you witness this persistence of segregation, the fragmentation, all these fights over resources, this finger-pointing. You would have to be blind not to see it."

It is a phenomenon sometimes difficult to measure, but not observe. Houses of worship remain, as the Rev. Martin Luther King Jr. described it three decades ago, among the most segregated institutions in America, not just by race but also ethnicity. At high school cafeterias, the second and third generation children of immigrants clump together in cliques defined by where their parents or grandparents were born. There are television sitcoms, talk shows and movies that are considered black or white, Latino or Asian. At a place like the law school of the University of California at Los Angeles, which has about 1,000 students, there are separate student associations for blacks, Latinos and Asians, with their own law review journals.

The Loss of Community

It almost goes without saying that today's new arrivals are a source of vitality and energy, especially in the big cities to which many are attracted. Diversity, almost everyone agrees, is good; choice is good; exposure to different cultures and ideas is good.

But many scholars worry about the loss of community and shared sense of reality among Americans, what Todd Gitlin, a professor of culture and communications at New York University, calls "the twilight of common dreams." The concern is echoed by many on both the left and right, and of all ethnicities, but no one seems to know exactly what to do about it.

Academics who examine the census data and probe for meaning in the numbers already speak of a new "demographic balkanization," not only of residential segregation, forced or chosen but also a powerful preference to see ourselves through a racial prism, wary of others, and, in many instances, hostile.

At a recent school board meeting in East Palo Alto, Calif., police had to break up a fight between Latinos and blacks, who were arguing over the merits and expense of bilingual education in a school district that has shifted over the last few years from majority African American to majority Hispanic. One parent told reporters that if the Hispanics wanted to learn Spanish they should stay in Mexico.

A Changing Population

The demographic shifts are smudging the old lines demarcating two historical, often distinct societies, one black and one white. Reshaped by three decades of rapidly rising immigration, the national story is now far more complicated.

Whites currently account for 74 percent of the population, blacks 12 percent, Hispanics 10 percent and Asians 3 percent. Yet according to data and predictions generated by the U.S. Census Bureau and social scientists poring over the numbers, Hispanics will likely surpass blacks early in the next century. And by the year 2050, demographers predict, Hispanics will account for 25 percent of the population, blacks 14 percent, Asians 8 percent, with whites hovering somewhere around 53 percent.

As early as 1999, whites no longer will be the majority in California; in Hawaii and New Mexico this is already the case. Soon after, Nevada, Texas, Maryland and New Jersey are also predicted to become "majority minority" states, entities where no one ethnic group remains the majority.

The overwhelming majority of immigrants come from Asia and Latin America—Mexico, the Central American countries, the Philippines, Korea, and Southeast Asia.

What triggered this great transformation was a change to immigration law in 1965, when Congress made family re-unification the primary criteria for admittance. That new policy, a response to charges that the law favored white Europeans, allowed immigrants already in the United States to bring over their relatives, who in turn could bring over more relatives. As a result, America has been absorbing as many as 1 million newcomers a year, to the point that now almost 1 in every 10 residents is foreign-born.

These numbers, relative to the overall population, were slightly higher at the beginning of the twentieth century, but the current immigration wave is in many ways very different, and its context inexorably altered, from the last great wave.

This time around, tensions are sharpened by the changing profile of those who are entering America's borders. Not only are their racial and ethnic backgrounds more varied than in decades past, their place in a modern postindustrial economy has also been recast.

The newly arrived today can be roughly divided into two camps: those with college degrees and highly specialized skills, and those with almost no education or job training.

Some 12 percent of immigrants have graduate degrees, compared with 8 percent of native Americans. But more than one-third of the immigrants have no high school diploma, double the rate for those born in the United States.

Before 1970, immigrants were actually doing better than natives overall, as measured by education, rate of homeownership and average incomes.

But those arriving after 1970 are younger, more likely to be underemployed and live below the poverty level. As a group, they are doing worse than natives.

About 6 percent of new arrivals receive some form of welfare, double the rate for U.S.-born citizens. Among some newcomers—Cambodians and Salvadorans, for example—the numbers are even higher.

With large numbers of immigrants arriving from Latin America, and segregating in barrios, there is also evidence of lingering language problems. Consider that in Miami, three-quarters of residents speak a language other than English at home, and 67 percent of those say they are not fluent in English. In New York City, 4 of every 10 residents speak a language other than English at home, and of these, half said they do not speak English well.

The New "White Flight"

It is clear that not all of America is experiencing the impact of immigration equally. Although even small Midwestern cities have seen sharp changes in their racial and ethnic mix in the past two decades, most immigrants continue to cluster into a handful of large, mostly coastal metropolitan areas: Los Angeles, New York, San Francisco, Chicago, Miami, Washington, D.C., and Houston. They are home to more than a quarter of the total U.S. population and more than 60 percent of all foreign-born residents.

But as the immigrants arrive, many American-born citizens pour out of these cities in search of new homes in more homogeneous locales. New York and Los Angeles each lost more than 1 million native-born residents between 1990 and 1995, even as their populations increased by roughly the same numbers with immigrants. To oversimplify, says University of Michigan demographer William Frey, "For every Mexican who comes to Los Angeles, a white native-born leaves."

Most of the people leaving the big cities are white and they tend to be working class. This is an entirely new kind of "white flight," whereby whites are not just fleeing the city centers for the suburbs but also are leaving the region, and often the state.

"The Ozzies and Harriets of the 1990s are skipping the suburbs of the big cities and moving to more homogeneous, mostly white smaller towns and smaller cities and rural areas," Frey says.

They're headed to Atlanta, Las Vegas, Phoenix, Portland, Denver, Austin and Orlando, as well as smaller cities in Nevada, Idaho, Colorado and Washington. Frey and other demographers believe the domestic migrants—black and white—are being "pushed" out, at least in part, by competition with immigrants for jobs and neighborhoods, political clout and lifestyle.

Frey sees in this pattern "the emergence of separate Americas, one white and middle-aged, less urban and another intensely urban, young, multicultural and multiethnic. One America will care deeply about English as the official language and about preserving Social Security. The other will care about things like retaining affirmative action and bilingual education."

Ethnic Segregation

Even within gateway cities that give the outward appearance of being multicultural, there are sharp lines of ethnic segregation. When describing the ethnic diversity of a bellwether megacity such as Los Angeles, many residents speak soaringly of the great mosaic of many peoples. But the social scientists who look at the hard census data see something more complex.

James P. Allen, a cultural geographer at California State University-Northridge, suggests that while Los Angeles, as seen from an airplane, is a tremendously mixed society, on the ground, racial homogeneity and segregation are common.

This is not a new phenomenon; there have always been immigrant neighborhoods. Ben Franklin, an early proponent of making English the "official language," worried about close-knit German communities. Democratic Sen.

Daniel Patrick Moynihan of New York described the lingering clannishness of Irish and other immigrant populations in New York in "Beyond the Melting Pot," a benchmark work from the 1960s that he wrote with Nathan Glazer.

Foreign-Born Americans

In 1960, foreign-born Americans were mostly from Europe. Now most come from Asia and Latin America.

1960		1996	
Germany	990,000	Mexico	6,679,000
Canada	963,000	Philippines	1,164,000
Poland	748,000	China	801,000
Soviet Union	691,000	Cuba	772,000
Mexico	576,000	India	757,000
England	528,000	Vietnam	740,000
Ireland	339,000	El Salvador	701,000
Austria	305,000	Canada	660,000
Hungary	245,000	Korea	550,000
Czechoslovakia	228,000	Germany	523,000

U.S. Census Bureau, 1996.

But the persistence of ethnic enclaves and identification does not appear to be going away, and may not in a country that is now home to not a few distinct ethnic groups, but to dozens. Hispanics in Los Angeles, to take the dominant group in the nation's second-largest city, were more segregated residentially in 1990 than they were 10 or 20 years ago, the census tracts show. Moreover, it is possible that what mixing of groups that does occur is only a temporary phenomenon as one ethnic group supplants another in the neighborhood.

Ethnic Labor Niches

If there is deep-seated ethnic segregation, it clearly extends to the American workplace. In many cities, researchers find sustained "ethnic niches" in the labor market. Because jobs are often a matter of whom one knows, the niches were enduring and remarkably resistant to outsiders.

In California, for example, Mexican immigrants are employed overwhelmingly as gardeners and domestics, in apparel and furniture manufacturing, and as cooks and food preparers. Koreans open small businesses. Filipinos become nurses and medical technicians. African Americans work in government jobs, an important niche that is increasingly being challenged by Hispanics who want in.

UCLA's Roger Waldinger and others have pointed to the creation, in cities of high immigration, of "dual economies."

For the affluent, which includes a disproportionate number of whites, the large labor pool provides them with a ready supply of gardeners, maids and nannies. For businesses in need of cheap manpower, the same is true. Yet there are fewer "transitional" jobs—the blue-collar work that helped Italian and Irish immigrants move up the economic ladder—to help newcomers or their children on their way to the jobs requiring advanced technical or professional skills that now dominate the upper tier of the economy.

The Mobility Trap

Traditionally, immigration scholars have seen the phenomenon of assimilation as a relentless economic progression. The hard-working new arrivals struggle along with a new language and at low-paying jobs in order for their sons and daughters to climb the economic ladder, each generation advancing a rung. There are many cases where this is true.

More recently, there is evidence to suggest that economic movement is erratic and that some groups—particularly in high immigration cities—can get "stuck."

Among African Americans, for instance, there emerge two distinct patterns. The black middle class is doing demonstrably better—in income, home ownership rates, education—than it was when the demographic transformation (and the civil rights movement) began three decades ago.

But for African Americans at the bottom, research indicates that immigration, particularly of Latinos with limited education, has increased joblessness and frustration.

In Miami, where Cuban immigrants dominate the political landscape, tensions are high between Hispanics and blacks, says Nathaniel J. Wilcox, a community activist there. "The perception in the black community, the reality, is that Hispanics don't want some of the power, they want all the power," Wilcox says. "At least when we were going through this with the whites during the Jim Crow era, at least they'd hire us. But Hispanics won't allow African Americans to even compete. They have this feeling that their community is the only community that counts."

Yet many Hispanics too find themselves in an economic "mobility trap." While the new immigrants are willing to work in low-end jobs, their sons and daughters, growing up in the barrios but exposed to the relentless consumerism of popular culture, have greater expectations, but are disadvantaged because of their impoverished settings, particularly the overwhelmed inner-city schools most immigrant children attend.

"One doubts that a truck-driving future will satisfy today's servants and assemblers. And this scenario gets a good deal more pessimistic if the region's economy fails to deliver or simply throws up more bad jobs," writes Waldinger, a professor of sociology and director of the center for regional policy studies at the University of California-Los Angeles. . . .

Resisting American Identity

Many immigrant parents say that although they want their children to advance economically in their new country, they do not want them to become "too American." A common concern among Haitians in South Florida is that their children will adopt the attitudes of the inner city's underclass. Vietnamese parents in New Orleans often try to keep their children immersed in their ethnic enclave and try not to let them assimilate too fast.

One study of the children of immigrants, conducted six years ago among young Haitians, Cubans, West Indians, Mexican and Vietnamese in South Florida and Southern California, suggests the parents are not alone in their concerns.

Asked by researchers Alejandro Portes and Ruben Rumbauthow how they identified themselves, most chose categories of hyphenated Americans. Few choose "American" as their identity.

Then there was this—asked if they believe the United States is the best country in the world, most of the youngsters answered: no.

"New immigrants are good for America."

Immigration Benefits America

Bill Clinton

America has been strengthened by wave after wave of immigrants, including the recent influx of Asian and Hispanic immigrants, states Bill Clinton in the following viewpoint. Most immigrants, he asserts, work hard and contribute much to America's culture and economy. Anti-immigrant sentiments and measures that attempt to exclude legal immigrants from American civic life are discriminatory and unfair, Clinton maintains. The United States must protect immigrants' rights to housing, education, and health care; in the meantime, immigrants must take on the task of becoming responsible American citizens. Clinton was the forty-second president of the United States. This viewpoint is excerpted from his commencement address at Portland State University, Oregon, on June 13, 1998.

As you read, consider the following questions:
1. According to Clinton, how many immigrants come to the United States each year?
2. Why is it wrong to condone illegal immigration, in the author's opinion?
3. What are the duties of citizenship, in Clinton's view?

Reprinted from Bill Clinton's commencement address at Portland State University, June 13, 1998.

Today I want to talk to you about what may be the most important subject of all—how we can strengthen the bonds of our national community as we grow more racially and ethnically diverse.

It was just in June 1997 that I launched a national initiative on race, asking Americans to address the persistent problems and the limitless possibilities of our diversity. This effort is especially important right now because, as we grow more diverse, our ability to deal with the challenges will determine whether we can really bind ourselves together as one America. And even more importantly in the near-term, and over the next few years, perhaps, as well, our ability to exercise world leadership for peace, for freedom, for prosperity in a world that is both smaller and more closely connected, and yet increasingly gripped with tense, often bloody conflicts rooted in racial, ethnic and religious divisions—our ability to lead that kind of world to a better place rests in no small measure on our ability to be a better place here in the United States that can be a model for the world.

The driving force behind our increasing diversity is a new, large wave of immigration. It is changing the face of America. And while most of the changes are good, they do present challenges which demand more both from new immigrants and from our citizens. Citizens share a responsibility to welcome new immigrants, to ensure that they strengthen our nation, to give them their chance at the brass ring.

In turn, new immigrants have a responsibility to learn, to work, to contribute to America. If both citizens and immigrants do their part, we will grow even stronger in the new global information economy.

Drawing Strength from Immigrants

More than any other nation on Earth, America has constantly drawn strength and spirit from wave after wave of immigrants. In each generation they have proved to be the most restless, the most adventurous, the most innovative, the most industrious of people. Bearing different memories, honoring different heritages, they have strengthened our economy, enriched our culture, renewed our promise of freedom and opportunity for all.

Of course, the path has not always run smooth. Some Americans have met each group of newcomers with suspicion and violence and discrimination. So great was the hatred of Irish immigrants 150 years ago that they were greeted with signs that read, "No Dogs Or Irish." So profound was the fear of Chinese in the 1880s that they were barred from entering the country. So deep was the distrust of immigrants from Southern and Eastern Europe at the beginning of [the twentieth] century that they were forced to take literacy tests specifically designed to keep them out of America.

Eventually the guarantees of our Constitution and the better angels of our nature prevailed over ignorance and insecurity, over prejudice and fear.

But now we are being tested again—by a new wave of immigration larger than any in a century, far more diverse than any in our history. Each year, nearly a million people come legally to America. Today, nearly one in ten people in America was born in another country; one in five schoolchildren is from immigrant families. Today, largely because of immigration, there is no majority race in Hawaii or Houston or New York City. Within five years there will be no majority race in our largest state, California. In a little more than 50 years there will be no majority race in the United States. No other nation in history has gone through demographic change of this magnitude in so short a time.

What do the changes mean? They can either strengthen and unite us, or they can weaken and divide us. We must decide.

Immigrants Are Good for America

Let me state my view unequivocally. I believe new immigrants are good for America. They are revitalizing our cities. They are building our new economy. They are strengthening our ties to the global economy, just as earlier waves of immigrants settled on the new frontier and powered the Industrial Revolution. They are energizing our culture and broadening our vision of the world. They are renewing our most basic values and reminding us all of what it truly means to be an American.

It means working hard, like a teenager from Vietnam who does his homework as he watches the cash register at his family's grocery store. It means making a better life for your children, like a father from Russia who works two jobs and still finds time to take his daughter to the public library to practice her reading. It means dreaming big dreams, passing them on to your children.

You have a lot of stories like that here at Portland State. Just this morning I met one of your graduates—or two, to be specific. Mago Gilson, an immigrant from Mexico who came here without a high school education. Twelve years later she is receiving her Master's Degree in education, on her way to realizing her dream of becoming a teacher.

She is joined in this class by her son Eddi, who had dreams of his own and worked full time for seven years to put himself through school. Today he receives a Bachelor's Degree in business administration. And soon—there's more. Soon her son Oscar, whom I also met, will receive his own Master's Degree in education. I'd like to ask the Gilsons and their family members who are here to rise and be recognized. There she is. Give them a hand.

The Spirit that Built America

In the Gilson family and countless like them, we see the spirit that built America—the drive to succeed, the commitment to family, to education, to work, the hope for a better life. In their stories we see a reflection of our parents' and grandparents' journey—a powerful reminder that our America is not so much a place as a promise; not a guarantee but a chance; not a particular race, but an embrace of our common humanity.

Now, some Americans don't see it that way. When they hear new accents or see new faces, they feel unsettled. They worry that new immigrants come not to work hard, but to live off our largesse. They're afraid the America they know and love is becoming a foreign land. This reaction may be understandable, but it's wrong. It's especially wrong when anxiety and fear give rise to policies and ballot propositions to exclude immigrants from our civic life. I believe it's wrong to deny law-abiding immigrants benefits available to everyone else;

wrong to ignore them as people not worthy of being counted on the census. It's not only wrong, it's un-American.

Let me be clear: I also think it's wrong to condone illegal immigration that flouts our laws, strains our tolerance, taxes our resources. Even a nation of immigrants must have rules and conditions and limits, and when they are disregarded, public support for immigration erodes in ways that are destructive to those who are newly arrived and those who are still waiting patiently to come.

We must remember, however, that the vast majority of immigrants are here legally. In every measurable way, they give more to our society than they take. Consider this: on average, immigrants pay $1,800 more in taxes every year than they cost our system in benefits. Immigrants are paying into Social Security at record rates. Most of them are young, and they will help to balance the budget when we baby boomers retire and put strains on it.

Sharing the Country

New immigrants also benefit the nation in ways not so easily measured, but very important. We should be honored that America, whether it's called the City on a Hill, or the Old Gold Mountain, or El Norte, is still seen around the world as the land of new beginnings. We should all be proud that people living in isolated villages in far corners of the world actually recognize the Statue of Liberty. We should rejoice that children the world over study our Declaration of Independence and embrace its creed.

My fellow Americans, we descendants of those who passed through the portals of Ellis Island must not lock the door behind us. Americans whose parents were denied the rights of citizenship simply because of the color of their skin must not deny those rights to others because of the country of their birth or the nature of their faith.

We should treat new immigrants as we would have wanted our own grandparents to be treated. We should share our country with them, not shun them or shut them out. But, mark my words, unless we handle this well, immigration of this sweep and scope could threaten the bonds of our union.

The Responsibilities of an American

Around the world we see what can happen when people who live on the same land put race and ethnicity before country and humanity. If America is to remain the world's most diverse democracy, if immigration is to strengthen America as it has throughout our history, then we must say to one another: whether your ancestors came here in slave ships or on the *Mayflower*; whether they landed on Ellis Island or at Los Angeles International Airport, or have been here for thousands of years, if you believe in the Declaration of Independence and the Constitution, if you accept the responsibilities as well as the rights embedded in them, then you are an American.

Respectful Pluralism

We each must make a commitment to a new respectful form of pluralism. . . . Our commitment must respect the history, the traditions, the culture, the literature, the values, the language and the music of Native Americans, African Americans, Latinos, Asian Pacific Americans and others as those cultural qualities have distinctly evolved within our borders. This modern vision recognizes that the Navajo's respect for the earth and its natural resources is an American value; that the African American–led civil rights movement of the 1960s represents a powerful movement in American history; that the folklore and labor of Mexican farm workers is an American experience; that the continuing nightmares of torture, death and heartache endured by Cambodian refugees and survivors of the Holocaust is a component of the American psyche. It recognizes that the American experience is broad and diverse.

Bill Ong Hing, *Poverty & Race*, January/February 1998.

Only that belief can keep us one America in the 21st century. So I say, as President, to all our immigrants, you are welcome here. But you must honor our laws, embrace our culture, learn our language, know our history; and when the time comes, you should become citizens. And I say to all Americans, we have responsibilities as well to welcome our newest immigrants, to vigorously enforce laws against discrimination. And I'm very proud that our nation's top civil rights enforcer is Bill Lam Lee, the son of Chinese immigrants who grew up in Harlem.

We must protect immigrants' rights and ensure their access to education, health care, and housing and help them to become successful, productive citizens. When immigrants take responsibility to become citizens and have met all the requirements to do so, they should be promptly evaluated and accepted.

The present delays in the citizenship process are unacceptable and indefensible. And together, immigrants and citizens alike, let me say we must recommit ourselves to the general duties of citizenship. Not just immigrants but every American should know what's in our Constitution and understand our shared history. Not just immigrants but every American should participate in our democracy by voting, by volunteering, and by running for office. Not just immigrants, but every American, on our campuses and in our communities, should serve—community service means good citizenship. And not just immigrants but every American should reject identity politics that seeks to separate us, not bring us together.

Ethnic pride is a very good thing. America is one of the places which most reveres the distinctive ethnic, racial, religious heritage of our various peoples. The days when immigrants felt compelled to Anglicize their last name or deny their heritage are, thankfully, gone. But pride in one's ethnic and racial heritage must never become an excuse to withdraw from the larger American community. That does not honor diversity; it breeds divisiveness. And that could weaken America.

The Importance of Education

Not just immigrants, but every American should recognize that our public schools must be more than places where our children learn to read, they must also learn to become good citizens. They must all be able to make America's heroes, from Washington to Lincoln to Eleanor Roosevelt and Rosa Parks and Cesar Chavez, their own.

Today, too many Americans, and far too many immigrant children, attend crowded, often crumbling, inner city schools.

Too many drop out of school altogether. And with more children from immigrant families entering our country and our schools than at any time since the turn of the [twentieth] century, we must renew our efforts to rebuild our schools and make them the best in the world. They must have better facilities; they must have smaller classes; they must have properly trained teachers; they must have access to technology; they must be the best in the world.

All of us, immigrants and citizens alike, must ensure that our new group of children learn our language, and we should find a way to do this together instead of launching another round of divisive political fights.

In the schools within just a few miles of the White House, across the Potomac River, we have the most diverse school district in America, where there are children from 180 different racial and ethnic groups, speaking as native tongues about 100 languages.

Now, it's all very well for someone to say, everyone of them should learn English immediately. But we don't at this time necessarily have people who are trained to teach them English in all those languages. So I say to you, it is important for children to retain their native language. But unless they also learn English, they will never reach their full potential in the United States.

Of course, English is learned at different rates, and, of course, children have individual needs. But that cannot be an excuse for making sure that when children come into our school system, we do whatever it takes with whatever resources are at hand to make sure they learn as quickly as they can the language that will be the dominant language of this country's commerce and citizenship in the future.

We owe it to these children to do that. And we should not either delay behind excuses or look for ways to turn what is essentially a human issue of basic decency and citizenship and opportunity into a divisive political debate. We have a stake together in getting together and moving forward on this.

Let me say, I applaud the students here at Portland State who are tutoring immigrant children to speak and read English. You are setting the kind of example I want our country to follow.

The Link Among Freedom-Loving People

One hundred and forty years ago, in the First Lady's hometown of Chicago, immigrants outnumbered native Americans. Addressing a crowd there in 1858, Abraham Lincoln asked what connection those immigrants could possibly feel to people like George Washington and Thomas Jefferson and John Adams, who founded our nation. Here was his answer: if they, the immigrants, look back through this history to trace their connection to those days by blood, they will find they have none. But our founders proclaimed that we are all created equal in the eyes of God. And that, Lincoln said, is the electric cord in that declaration that links the hearts of patriotic and liberty-loving people everywhere.

Well, that electric cord, the conviction that we are all created equal in the eyes of God, still links every graduate here with every new immigrant coming to our shores and every American who ever came before us. If you carry it with conscience and courage into the new century, it will light our way to America's greatest days—your days.

So, members of the Class of 1998, go out and build the future of your dreams. Do it together, for your children, for your grandchildren, for your country.

Good luck, and God bless you.

> "*Multiculturalism and the United States government's immigration policy have contributed toward the rise of Chicano ethnic separatism.*"

Immigration from Mexico Encourages Ethnic Conflict

Maria Hsia Chang

Maria Hsia Chang is a political science professor at the University of Nevada in Reno. In the following viewpoint, Chang contends that a growing number of Chicanos (Mexican-Americans) are refusing to become a part of mainstream American society and are fueling interethnic tensions. Many Chicanos, she points out, reject the U.S.–Mexican border that was set up in 1848 and insist that the American Southwest is really Mexico. Emboldened by radical political activists, multiculturalism, and the current influx of Latino immigrants, Chicano nationalists resist assimilation and seek to "reclaim" the Southwest as their homeland. This refusal to assimilate, coupled with the low level of educational and economic achievement among Chicanos, aggravates interethnic hostilities, Chang concludes.

As you read, consider the following questions:

1. What is Aztlan, according to Chang?
2. How do Chicanos differ from previous waves of immigrants, in the author's opinion?
3. What is the high-school dropout rate for U.S. Latinos, according to Chang?

Reprinted from "Multiculturalism, Immigration, and Aztlan," by Maria Hsia Chang, *The Social Contract*, Spring 2000. Reprinted with permission from *The Social Contract*.

One of the standard arguments invoked by those in favor of massive immigration into the United States is that our country is founded on immigrants who have always been successfully assimilated into America's mainstream culture and society. As one commentator put it, "Assimilation evokes the misty past of Ellis Island, through which millions entered, eventually seeing their descendants become as American as George Washington."

Nothing more vividly testifies against that romantic faith in America's ability to continuously assimilate new members than the events of October 16, 1994 in Los Angeles. On that day, 70,000 people marched beneath "a sea of Mexican flags" protesting Proposition 187, a referendum measure that would deny many state benefits to illegal immigrants and their children. [This measure was eventually declared unconstitutional.] Two weeks later, more protestors marched down the street, this time carrying an American flag upside down. Both protests point to a disturbing and rising phenomenon of Chicano separatism in the United States—the product of a complex of forces, among which are multiculturalism and a generous immigration policy combined with a lax border control.

The Problem

Chicanos refer to "people of Mexican descent in the United States" or "Mexican Americans in general." Today, there are reasons to believe that Chicanos as a group are unlike previous immigrants in that they are more likely to remain unassimilated and unintegrated, whether by choice or circumstance—resulting in the formation of a separate quasi-nation within the United States. More than that, there are Chicano political activists who intend to marry cultural separateness with territorial and political self-determination. The more moderate among them aspire to the cultural and political autonomy of "home rule." The radicals seek nothing less than secession from the United States whether to form their own sovereign state or to reunify with Mexico. Those who desire reunification with Mexico are irredentists who seek to reclaim Mexico's "lost" territories in the American Southwest. Whatever their goals, what animates all of them is the dream of Aztlan.

According to legend, Aztlan was the ancestral homeland of the Aztecs which they left in journeying southward to found Tenochtitlan, the center of their new civilization, which is today's Mexico City. Today, the "Nation of Aztlan" refers to the American southwestern states of California, Arizona, Texas, New Mexico, portions of Nevada, Utah, Colorado, which Chicano nationalists claim were stolen by the United States and must be reconquered *(Reconquista)* and reclaimed for Mexico. The myth of Aztlan was revived by Chicano political activists in the 1960s as a central symbol of Chicano nationalist ideology. In 1969, at the Chicano National Liberation Youth Conference in Denver, Rodolfo "Corky" Gonzales put forth a political document entitled El Plan de Aztlan (Spiritual Plan of Aztlan). The Plan is a clarion call to Mexican-Americans to form a separate Chicano nation:

> In the spirit of a new people that is conscious not only of its proud historical heritage, but also of the brutal "gringo " invasion of our territories, we, the Chicano inhabitants and civilizers of the northern land of Aztlan from whence came our forefathers . . . declare that the call of our blood is . . . our inevitable destiny. . . . Aztlan belongs to those who plant the seeds, water the fields, and gather the crops, and not to the foreign Europeans. We do not recognize capricious frontiers on the bronze continent. . . . Brotherhood unites us, and love for our brothers makes us a people whose Time has come. . . . With our heart in our hands and our hands in the soil, we declare the independence of our mestizo nation. We are a bronze people with a bronze culture. Before the world, before all of North America, before all our brothers in the bronze continent, we are a nation, we are a union of free pueblos, we are Aztlan.

Chicanos Are Unlike Previous Immigrants

Brent A. Nelson writing in 1994, observed that in the 1980s America's Southwest had begun to be transformed into a *de facto* nation with its own culture, history, myth, geography, religion, education and language. Whatever evidence there is indicates that Chicanos, as a group, are unlike previous waves of immigrants into the United States.

In the first place, many Chicanos do not consider themselves immigrants at all because their people "have been here for 450 years" before the English, French, or Dutch. Before

California and the Southwest were seized by the United States, they were the lands of Spain and Mexico. As late as 1780 the Spanish crown laid claim to territories from Florida to California, and on the far side of the Mississippi up to the Great Lakes and the Rockies. Mexico held title to much of Spanish possessions in the United States until the Treaty of Guadalupe Hidalgo ended the Mexican-American war in 1848. As a consequence, Mexicans "never accepted the borders drawn up by the 1848 treaty."

That history has created among Chicanos a feeling of resentment for being "a conquered people," made part of the United States against their will and by the force of arms. Their resentment is amply expressed by *Voz Fronteriza*, a Chicano student publication, which referred to Border Patrol officers killed in the line of duty as "pigs *(migra)*" trying to defend "the false frontier."

Chicanos are also distinct from other immigrant groups because of the geographic proximity of their native country. Their physical proximity to Mexico gives Chicanos "the option of life in both Americas, in two places and in two cultures, something earlier immigrants never had." Geographic proximity and ease of transportation are augmented by the media. Radio and television keep the spoken language alive and current so that Spanish, unlike the native languages of previous immigrants into the United States, "shows no sign of fading."

A result of all that is the failure by Chicanos to be fully assimilated into the larger American society and culture. As Earl Shorris, author of *Latinos: A Biography of the People*, observed: "Latinos have been more resistant to the melting pot than any other group. Their entry *en masse* into the United States will test the limits of the American experiment. . . ." The continuous influx of Mexican immigrants into the United States serves to continuously renew Chicano culture so that their sense of separateness will probably continue "far into the future. . . ."

Why Chicanos Fail to Assimilate

There are other reasons for the failure of Chicano assimilation. Historically, a powerful force for assimilation was upward social mobility—immigrants into the United States became assimilated as they rose in educational achievement and income. But today's post-industrial American economy, with its narrower paths to upward mobility, is making it more difficult for certain groups to improve their socioeconomic circumstances. Unionized factory jobs, which once provided a step up for the second generation of past waves of immigrants, have been disappearing for decades.

The Legend of Aztlan

[There is an] irredentist fantasy that California, Arizona, New Mexico, Colorado, and Texas—the states created in the territory obtained from Mexico through the Treaty of Guadalupe Hidalgo in 1848—compose "Aztlan," the mythical homeland of the Aztec Indians, and that those states must be wrested from the United States in order to create a new Chicano homeland. More than a quarter of a century ago, political analyst Patty Newman warned that "the basic concept of El Plan de Aztlan is endorsed by most of the major Mexican-American organizations on campus and off, liberal and supposedly conservative." Believers in the Aztlan legend insist upon the indivisibility of "*la Raza*" (the Mexican race) and the need to abolish the border between the U.S. and Mexico; one of their preferred slogans is, "We didn't cross the border—the border crossed us."

William Norman Grigg, *New American*, February 19, 1996.

Instead of the diamond-shaped economy of industrial America, the modern American economy is shaped like an hourglass. There is a good number of jobs for unskilled people at the bottom, a fair number of jobs for the highly educated at the top, but comparatively few jobs for those in the middle without a college education or special skills. To illustrate, a RAND Corporation study forecasts that 85 percent of California's new jobs will require post-secondary education.

For a variety of reasons, the nationwide high-school dropout rate for Hispanics (the majority of whom are Chicano) is 30 percent—three times the rate for whites and twice the rate for blacks. Paradoxically, the dropout rate for Hispanics born in the United States is even higher than for young immigrants. Among Chicanos, high-school dropout rates actually rise between the second and third generations.

Their low educational achievement accounts for why Chicanos as a group are poor despite being hardworking. In 1996, for the first time, the Hispanic poverty rate began to exceed that of American blacks. In 1995, household income rose for every ethnic group except Hispanics, for whom it dropped 5 percent. Latinos now make up a quarter of the nation's poor people, and are more than three times as likely to be impoverished than whites. This decline in income has taken place despite high rates of labor-force participation by Latino men, and despite an emerging Latino middle class. In California, where Latinos now approach one-third of the population, their education levels are far lower than those of other immigrants, and they earn about half of what native-born Californians earn. This means that, for the first time in the history of American immigration, hard work is not leading to economic advancement because immigrants in service jobs face unrelenting labor-market pressure from more recently arrived immigrants who are eager to work for less.

The narrowing of the pathways of upward mobility has implications for the children of recent Mexican immigrants. Their ascent into the middle-class mainstream will likely be blocked and they will join children of earlier black and Puerto Rican migrants as part of an expanded multiethnic underclass. Whereas first generation immigrants compare their circumstances to the Mexico that they left—and thereby feel immeasurably better off—their children and grandchildren will compare themselves to other U.S. groups. Given their lower educational achievement and income, that comparison will only lead to feelings of relative deprivation and resentment. They are unlikely to be content as maids, gardeners, or fruit pickers. Many young Latinos in the second and third generations see themselves as locked in irremediable conflict with white society, and are quick to deride successful Chicano students as "wannabes." For them, to study hard is to "act white" and exhibit group disloyalty.

The Chicano Culture of Resistance

That attitude is part of the Chicano culture of resistance—a culture that actively resists assimilation into mainstream

America. That culture is created, reinforced, and maintained by radical Chicano intellectuals, politicians, and the many Chicano Studies programs in U.S. colleges and universities.

As examples, according to its editor, Elizabeth Martinez, the purpose of *Five Hundred Years of Chicano History*, a book used in over 300 schools throughout the West, is to "celebrate our resistance to being colonized and absorbed by racist empire builders." The book calls the INS and the Border Patrol "the Gestapo for Mexicans." For Rodolfo Acuña, author of *Occupied America: The Chicano's Struggle Toward Liberation*, probably the most widely-assigned text in U.S. Chicano Studies programs, the Anglo-American invasion of Mexico was "as vicious as that of Hitler's invasion of Poland and other Central European nations. . . ." The book also includes a map showing "the Mexican republic" in 1822 reaching up into Kansas and Oklahoma, and including within it Utah, Nevada, and everything west and south of there. At a MEChA conference in 1996, Acuña referred to Anglos as Nazis: "Right now you are in the Nazi United States of America."

The effect of books such as these is to radicalize young Chicanos. As an example, although Chicano undergraduates at Berkeley lacked any sort of strong ethnic identity before entering college, at Berkeley they became "born again" as Chicanos because of MEChA and Chicano Studies departments.

The strident rhetoric of intellectuals is echoed by some Mexican-American politicians. Former California state senator Art Torres called Proposition 187 "the last gasp of white America" and spoke of "reclaiming" Southern California. The Mexican government also contributes to the Chicano sense of separateness through its recent decision that migrants will not forfeit their Mexican citizenship by becoming U.S. citizens and are allowed to vote in Mexican elections.

Multiculturalism and Immigration

All of this is exacerbated by the U.S. government's immigration policy and a new ethic of multiculturalism that has become almost an official dogma in the mass media and in academe. Exponents of multiculturalism maintain that all cultures are equal, and that the United States must accept its destiny as a universal nation, a world nation, in which no one culture—especially European culture—will be dominant. "The ideal of multiculturalism is a notion which has no core culture, no ethnic core, no center other than a powerful state apparatus."

The social ethic of multiculturalism is actively supported by an official government policy of "corporate pluralism" which militates against America's earlier ideal of assimilation. According to Gunnar Myrdal, "corporate pluralism" refers to a society where racial and ethnic entities are accorded formal recognition and standing by the state as groups in the national polity, and where political power and economic reward are based on a distributive formula that postulates group rights and defines group membership as an important factor in the outcome for individuals. By replacing individual meritocracy with group rewards, corporate pluralism "strongly discourages assimilation in the conventional sense because if a significant portion of one's rational interests are likely to be satisfied by emphasis on one's ethnicity, then one might as well stay within ethnic boundaries and at the same time enjoy the social comforts of being among people of one's own kind."

Corporate pluralism is realized through such government policies as affirmative action, court-ordered busing, and bilingual education. In the case of the latter, by the late 1970s, bilingual education has become "a Hispanic institution." A bilingual establishment has been formed which "fights for jobs and perks" and is determined to maintain Spanish as both language and culture. Being supported by government laws, that establishment cannot easily be dislodged.

The Growing Chicano Population

Chicanos are not the only ethnic group in the United States who resist assimilation and are geographically concentrated in certain areas and cities. The Cubans in Miami and Chinese in Monterey Park are other examples, but neither group is large enough to practice autonomism or separatism. Chicanos in the Southwest, however, are great in numbers and "are producing spokesmen for . . . autonomism, separatism, and even irredentism."

Since 1977, INS has apprehended over a million illegals a

year, the majority Hispanics; anywhere from 2 to 5 million eluded the INS. By the early 1980s, the number of illegal aliens in the United States, mostly Hispanic, totaled 3 to 12 million. In 1980, the Census Bureau counted 14.6 million Hispanics in the United States, increasing to 15.8 million by 1982, and 17.3 million by 1985—making America the 5th or 4th largest Spanish-speaking country in the world. According to the 1990 Census, Latin America accounted for 38 percent of America's foreign-born, well over half of whom were from Mexico. The real percentage is probably higher because illegal aliens avoid the census and most illegals are from Latin America.

According to a report by the Urban Institute in 1984 entitled *The Fourth Wave: California's Newest Immigrants*, by the year 2000, 42 percent of Southern California's residents will be Caucasian, 41 percent Hispanic, 9 percent Asian and 8 percent black. Demographers Leon F. Bouvier and Cary B. Davis in *Immigration and the Future Racial Composition of the United States* expect that, by 2080, Hispanics (more than half Chicano) will constitute 34.1 percent of the total U.S. population, even if immigration were restricted to 2 million entrants a year from all areas of the world and birthrates of Hispanics converge with those of non-Hispanics. In 2080, Hispanics will be either a plurality or a majority of the population in California and Texas at 41.4 percent and 53.5 percent, respectively, assuming an influx of a conservative one million immigrants a year.

El Plan de Aztlan

Former Senator Eugene McCarthy, writing in 1987, had warned of a "recolonization." McCarthy's warning was sounded five years earlier by a historian of race relations, George Fredrickson. Speaking at a colloquium on race relations in 1982, Fredrickson observed that:

> There are two ways that you can gain territory from another group. One is by conquest. That's essentially the way we took California from Mexico and . . . Texas as well. But what's going on now may well end up being a kind of recolonization of the Southwest, because the other way you can regain territory is by population infiltration and demographic dominance. . . . The United States will be faced with

the problem that Canada has been faced with . . . and which our system is not prepared to accommodate.

Mario Barrera, a faculty member of UC Berkeley's Department of Ethnic Studies, admitted that multiculturalism "would help prepare the ideological climate for an eventual campaign for ethnic regional autonomy." In January 1995, El Plan de Aztlan Conference at UC Riverside resolved that "We shall overcome . . . by the vote if possible and violence if necessary." The rise of Mexican irredentism as a serious political movement "awaits only the demographic transformation of the Southwest. As an article entitled "The Great Invasion: Mexico Recovers Its Own" in a 1982 edition of *Excelsior*, Mexico's leading daily newspaper, put it:

> The territory lost in the 19th century by . . . Mexico . . . seems to be restoring itself through a humble people who go on settling various zones that once were ours on the old maps. Land, under any concept of possession, ends up in the hands of those who deserve it. . . . [The result of this migration is to return the land] to the jurisdiction of Mexico without the firing of a single shot.

Multiculturalism and the United States government's immigration policy have contributed toward the rise of Chicano ethnic separatism within the American Southwest that has all the makings of an incipient Nation of Aztlan.

"Suburbs are no longer simply the settling place for white flight from the cities, they are emergent racial battlefields."

Nativism Among Whites Encourages Ethnic Conflict

Mike Davis and Alessandra Moctezuma

Nativism and anti-immigrant sentiment among whites is contributing to interracial conflict in the United States, contend Mike Davis and Alessandra Moctezuma in the following viewpoint. The militarization of the U.S.–Mexico border—which has led to the inhumane treatment of Latino migrant workers—is rooted in this nativism, the authors argue. Moreover, the emergence of certain kinds of residential barriers in American suburbs reveals anti-Hispanic prejudice among whites. Latinos living in the Los Angeles area, for example, are finding that blockaded streets and high fees for the use of recreational parks often segregate them from whites. Davis is an award-winning author; Moctezuma is a muralist, artist, and writer.

As you read, consider the following questions:
1. According to Davis and Moctezuma, what is Operation Gatekeeper?
2. What is the U.S. Border Patrol's "second line of defense," according to the authors?
3. According to the authors, how did the San Marino city council respond to the appearance of Latinos in one of the city parks?

Reprinted from "Policing the Third Border," by Mike Davis and Alessandra Moctezuma, *Colorlines*, Fall 1999. Reprinted with permission from *Colorlines*.

All borders are acts of state violence inscribed in landscape. Every wall and fence, checkpoint and pillbox, is a sundering of the integrity of nature and the rights of man. The very existence of exclusionary borders, as all great radical thinkers have understood, constitutes a permanent crisis of human liberty.

Borders are also historically specific social systems, which frequently shape distinctive borderland cultures and identities. They spill over in all directions. Borders are thus incomparably messier and more complex than our comforting image of precise black lines on maps.

Over the course of 150 years, the U.S.–Mexican border has grown sadistic teeth of razor wire and concrete, reinforced by state-of-the-art surveillance technology and a stealth army of border police. At the same time, the border has penetrated daily life far north and south of *la linea* itself. Its ramifications have become complex and despotic. Increasingly, we need to distinguish three separate but interrelated systems of cultural control, each expressed in a distinctive landscape.

Primera Frontera

The first border, of course, commemorates the 1847 war of aggression by an expansionist slave republic (U.S.) against its peaceful, non-slaveholding neighbor (Mexico). The war against Mexico was condemned by every contemporary American of conscience, from Henry David Thoreau (who went to jail in protest) to Ulysses S. Grant (who later renounced his participation as "immoral"). More importantly, its legitimacy has never been acknowledged by those communities whose lives and histories it cleaved. "We didn't cross the border, it crossed us," shouted Latino students in recent protests against anti-immigrant legislation in California.

In the nineteenth century, however, the border was often difficult to locate. From the Treaty of Guadalupe Hidalgo, which ended the U.S. invasion of Mexico in 1848, until the Mexican Revolution of 1910, the international border west of the Rio Grande consisted only of occasional stone monuments shaped like squat obelisks and laid out by survey teams in the 1850s. It was a geopolitical fiction that barely intruded into the daily existence of the largely pastoral communities of mestizo and indigenous people thinly sprinkled across the Sonoran Desert. Longhorned cattle, copper miners, Apache raiding parties, and their U.S. and Mexican pursuers crossed the invisible line at will.

The Mexican Revolution of 1910 and subsequent U.S. attempts to manipulate its outcome led to the initial militarization of the border. The U.S. Army was sent into the Rio Grande valley, New Mexico, and Arizona, and U.S. sailors and marines occupied Mexico's major ports. While "Black Jack" Pershing's cavalry vainly chased Pancho Villa's *dorados* across Chihuahua, barbed wire divided families in frontier towns and ranchos for the first time. In the 1920s, the Border Patrol was created to replace the Army in this task. Yet the new system of "border control," while designed to keep revolutionary ideas and intrigues out of Texas and the Southwest, was never intended to stop the flow of labor northward.

On the contrary, the abrupt decline in European mass immigration after the outbreak of the First World War created a rising demand for Mexican workers, especially in California. The border was reconceptualized as a dam, pooling a reservoir of cheap, disposable labor along *La Frontera* that could be pumped as needed to U.S. fields, households, and sweatshops. As *braceros* during the 1940s and 1950s or as *mojados* (undocumented immigrants), Mexican laborers were deprived of any formal right of organization or freedom of speech. When their numbers temporarily became too great (as in Los Angeles County during the Depression) or when they persisted in organizing militant unions (as in the Imperial Valley in 1949–50), they were simply deported.

Today, the role of the border is still to reinforce the extra-economic coercion of immigrant labor in the non-union sectors of the U.S. economy. Since 1996, the Clinton Administration has dramatically increased the militarization of the border, doubling the size of the Border Patrol while reintroducing ("in supportive roles") National Guard, Army, and Marine troops in the largest numbers since 1917.

The War on Drugs, whose principal battleground has now been officially shifted from the Andes to the U.S.–Mexico border, has been used to justify such draconian programs as Operation Gatekeeper which, through a combination of technology and sheer manpower, aims to stanch all illegal flows through San Ysidro, the world's busiest border crossing between San Diego and Tijuana. While neither drugs nor immigration have been significantly deterred, at least 340 people who were diverted by Operation Gatekeeper to the remote desert and mountain areas have died of thirst and exposure since 1994.

Segunda Frontera

As long ago as the 1940s, the Border Patrol experimented with a "second line of defense," composed of automobile dragnets inland from the international border. In the 1960s, with the construction of several interstate highways linking the Los Angeles region with the border, the Immigration and Naturalization Service established permanent checkpoints and detention facilities. The most notorious is on Interstate 5 (I-5) at San Onofre, 75 miles north of the border, near Richard Nixon's former "Western White House." The great river of traffic flowing between San Diego and Orange counties is inspected 24 hours a day. "Suspicious" vehicles, often carrying Latino U.S. citizens, are regularly pulled over and searched.

To bypass the Border Patrol, coyotes (smugglers) unload their passengers a mile or so south of the checkpoint. The undocumented immigrants—tired, scared, and usually unfamiliar with freeways—are ordered to cross ten lanes of 70-mph traffic to the west side of I-5, then make their way down to the beach (part of the huge Camp Pendleton Marine Base) and head north to an eventual rendezvous point. Even in the small hours of the morning, gaps in the traffic flow are infrequent and crossing I-5 is always extremely dangerous. In the last twenty years, several hundred immigrants, including entire families holding hands, have been mowed down. At one point, there was a special therapy group in San Diego for drivers who had accidentally killed freeway crossers.

After spending a million dollars studying every option, except closing the checkpoint, California's transportation authority—CalTrans—created the world's first official Pedestrian Accident Zone in the late 1980s, replete with bizarre warning signs that depict a family bolting across the highway. It was a moral threshold in the naturalization of the unnatural and inhumane. It is a perfect symbol for a new North American free trade system that promotes the free movement of capital while turning migrant laborers into pariahs.

Tercera Frontera

In Southern California, a third border has also emerged in recent years. As the Latino population of Los Angeles and Orange Counties has burgeoned to nearly five million in the mid-1990s, architectural and legal barriers have been constructed at precisely those points where blue-collar Chicano or new immigrant communities connect with upper-income Anglo communities. Whereas the second border nominally reinforces the international border, the third border polices daily intercourse between two citizen communities.

Although other instances abound in suburban Southern California, we have documented the third border in the San Gabriel Valley of Los Angeles County. Once the center of the California citrus industry, the San Gabriel Valley is a mature, built-out suburban landscape with 1.8 million residents. It is politically fragmented into more than forty shards, ranging from large secondary cities like Pasadena and Pomona to unincorporated county "islands" and special-use incorporations like the eponymous City of Industry.

Although the great orchards were subdivided into tract homes a half century ago, the citrus era left a legacy that continues to frame all social relations in the Valley: a fundamental division between a Chicano/Mexicano working class and an Anglo upper middle class. The traditional demographic balance, however, has been overturned. Chicano residents now outnumber Anglos by roughly three to two, and there is a growing Chicano managerial-professional class. Further, an influx of about 250,000 Chinese has given rise to a spectacular eight-mile-long linear Chinatown in the suburbs of Monterey Park, Alhambra, and San Gabriel.

Although many blue-collar Anglo residents have exited the southern tier of Valley towns where they were formerly the majority, the traditionally wealthy tier of foothill communities from Pasadena to Claremont remains highly attractive to young white professionals as well as to traditional elites. Here are the sharpest ethnic and class tensions. The function of the third border is to separate these two populations, to restrict Latino use of public space such as streets, shopping districts, and parks.

Suburban Barricades

Take, for example, the boundary between El Sereno and South Pasadena. El Sereno is a protrusion of the City of Los Angeles into the western San Gabriel Valley. It is a well-groomed, blue-collar suburb, home to hardworking truckdrivers, medical secretaries, and postal workers. Most have last names like Hernández or Rodríguez. South Pasadena, on the other hand, is a separately incorporated small town, renowned for its big Midwestern-style homes, tree-lined streets, and first class schools. Its median home values are at least $100,000 higher than El Sereno's.

The Core of Xenophobia

Fear is at the core of xenophobia. This fear is particularly disturbing when it is directed at the most vulnerable victims: migrant workers. They become the "invaders" from the south, the human incarnation of the Mexican fly, the sub-human "wetbacks," the "aliens" from another (cultural) planet. They are always suspected of stealing "our jobs," of shrinking "our budget," of taking advantage of the welfare system, of not paying taxes, and of bringing disease, drugs, street violence, foreign thoughts, pagan rites, primitive customs, and alien sounds. Their indigenous features and rough clothes remind uninformed citizens of an unpleasant pre–European American past and of mythical lands to the south immersed in poverty and political turmoil, where innocent gringos could be attacked for no apparent reason. Yet these invaders no longer inhabit the remote past, a banana republic, or a Hollywood film. They actually live down the block, and their children go to the same schools as do the Anglo kids.

Guillermo Gómez-Peña, *Utne Reader*, September/October 1995.

Some years ago, the South Pasadena city fathers decided that the twain must never meet and engineered the barricading of busy Van Horne Street. To those on its "bad side," this new border signifies the stigmatization of their neighborhood. Serenos were especially incensed when South Pasadena justified the street closure in the name of "preventing drive-by shootings." Since many older Chicanos tell stories of decades of harassment by the South Pasadena police, it is not surprising that they regard the barricade in the same way black southerners once felt about segregated drinking fountains.

Ricardo Mirelles Córdova, who lives on "the wrong side" of the barricaded street between South Pasadena and El Sereno, asks: "How would you like your neighborhood and property values defined by being on 'the wrong side' of the local equivalent of the Berlin Wall?" Raquel Sánchez wryly retorts: "I actually kind of like the border. It keeps all those speeding Lexuses and BMWs off our side so that the kids can play safely on the street."

A group of affluent homeowners in nearby Duarte, meanwhile, are lobbying the city to allow them to install a guardhouse at the entrance to their foothill subdivision. The purpose of the checkpoint would be to discourage "suspicious persons who do not belong in the neighborhood." Latinos in Duarte, up in arms over the incipient privatization of a public street, have protested that they and their children are, in fact, the object of this paranoia.

Internal Borderlands

Parks have become another internal borderland. Ironically, for an area that once exulted in its orchards and wild mountains, there is now an acute recreation crisis in the San Gabriel Valley. It has been generated by the failure of postwar developments to set aside adequate park space and compounded by declining revenues in the wake of Proposition 13. For affluent families on quiet, palm-lined streets in the foothill belt, there is no real problem. But Latino apartment dwellers in the tractlands along the freeways usually have to leave their own neighborhood to find space for a Sunday picnic under a shady oak tree. Increasingly, however, they find signs telling them that they are not welcome.

San Marino is the richest city in the Valley and one of the wealthiest in the nation. It embalms ancient regional dynasties like the Chandlers of the *L.A. Times* and formerly provided a headquarters to the John Birch Society. In recent years, some of the housecleaners and gardeners who keep its lush lifestyle scrubbed and well-pruned started bringing their own families to San Marino's beautiful Lacy Park on weekends. But the appearance of "aliens" in their cherished park incited near hysteria on the San Marino city council.

The council's response was to impose a weekend-use fee for non-residents. Twelve dollars for a family of four is no deterrent to wealthy visitors, but it is too steep for San Marino's low-paid workers and their kids. (The council, incredibly, justified the fee by claiming that the city was nearly broke.) Meanwhile, San Marino's crown jewel, the world-famous Huntington Library and Gardens, built on the surplus value of Henry Huntington's Mexican track laborers, changed its long-time "donation requested" to a strictly enforced eight dollar per head admission—another deterrent to diversity amidst the azaleas.

The Return of Nativism

Arcadia, home of the famous Santa Anita racetrack, also has a bad reputation amongst Valley Latinos. Historically, it was one of the few citrus-belt towns that refused to allow its Mexican workers to live anywhere in the city limits, even on the other side of the tracks. In 1939, 99 percent of its burghers signed a unique "covenant." Organized by a local escrow company, it promised to keep their piece of paradise "Caucasian forever." They have never given up trying.

When Arcadia's Wilderness Park became popular with Spanish-speaking families in the early 1990s, nativism reared its ugly head. One leader of the neighboring Highland Oaks Homeowner's Association complained: "I've seen their graffiti. I've heard their ghetto blasters. I don't want any riffraff coming into our city." Then-mayor Joseph Ciraulo, agreed: "The park has been overrun with these people." As a result, Arcadia restricted public use of the park, now officially a "wilderness center," to a single eight-hour period on Fridays.

Similar complaints about "noise," "gangbangers," and "graffiti" recently led county officials to accede to the wishes of the wealthy residents of the east Altadena area and ban weekend parking near trailheads and canyons on the flank of famous Mount Wilson. Again, the ban followed a rise in recreational use by low-income Latinos and African Americans.

Crabgrass Apartheid

In effect, well-heeled Valley communities, long accused of discriminatory policing, are now corporately privatizing recreational space. The NIMBY ("Not In My Backyard!") politics of residential exclusionism are rapidly fusing with the new nativism to create a third border distant from, but complimentary to, the first and second borders. While the other borders are meant to exclude Mexican immigrants from entry into the U.S., the third border serves as a new form of racial segregation deep within the country. Suburbs are no longer simply the settling place for white flight from the cities, they are emergent racial battlefields.

This crabgrass apartheid, represented by blockaded streets and off-limits parks, should be as intolerable as Jim Crow drinking fountains or segregated schools were in the 1960s. For Latinos, supposedly on the threshold of majority power in Los Angeles County, citizenship will never be fully achieved until this third border is dismantled.

Periodical Bibliography

The following articles have been selected to supplement the diverse views presented in this chapter. Addresses are provided for periodicals not indexed in the *Readers' Guide to Periodical Literature*, the *Alternative Press Index*, the *Social Sciences Index*, or the *Index to Legal Periodicals and Books*.

Michael Barone — "How Hispanics Are Americanizing," *Wall Street Journal*, February 6, 1998.

Arian Campo-Flores — "Brown Against Brown," *Newsweek*, September 18, 2000.

Linda Chavez — "Our Hispanic Predicament," *Commentary*, June 1998.

Michael A. Fletcher — "All Fighting for a Piece of the Dream," *Washington Post National Weekly Edition*, May 18, 1998. Available from 1150 15th St. NW, Washington, DC 20071.

Samuel G. Freedman — "Wave of Hate Crimes Reflects a War Against Immigrants," *USA Today*, August 24, 1999.

Elaine M. Kim — "'At Least You're Not Black': Asian Americans in U.S. Race Relations," *Social Justice*, Fall 1998.

George Lipsitz — "Why Inter-Ethnic Anti-Racism Matters Now," *Colorlines*, Winter 1999.

Ying Ma — "Black Racism," *American Enterprise*, November/December 1998. Available from 1150 17th St. NW, Washington, DC 20036.

Elizabeth Martinez — "It's a Terrorist War on Immigrants," *Z Magazine*, July/August 1997.

Scott McConnell — "Americans No More?" *National Review*, December 31, 1997.

Ana Radelat — "Banned at the Border," *Hispanic*, January 1998. Available from the Hispanic Publishing Corporation, 98 San Jacinto Blvd., Ste. 1150, Austin, TX 78701.

Danny Widener — "The World is Waiting for the Sunrise: African Americans *y el Mundo Latino*," *Social Justice*, Fall 1998.

CHAPTER 3

How Has Affirmative Action Affected Race Relations?

Chapter Preface

Since the 1960s, the U.S. government has endorsed affirmative action to counteract the effects of discrimination on women and minorities. Affirmative action policies increase female and minority representation in the workforce and in public university populations—typically by including race and gender as factors in hiring and college admissions decisions. Critics, however, maintain that the use of any kind of racial preference is a form of discrimination. Many point to a situation at the University of Texas Law School as recent proof that affirmative action is unfair. Four white students sued the law school in 1992, claiming that they had been denied admission so that less-qualified minorities could attend the school. As a result of this lawsuit, the school was required to reveal its 1992 entrance exam scores. Minority students with lower test scores had in fact been admitted to the detriment of some white students with higher scores. This, prosecutors maintained, was reverse discrimination, and an appeals court ruled that the law school could no longer elevate some races over others in its admissions policies.

Affirmative action supporters, however, argue that test scores should be only one out of many criteria for selecting students. As former university presidents William G. Bowen and Derek Bok attest, "Colleges do not automatically offer admission as a reward for past performance to anyone. Nor should they." Hard-to-test qualities such as determination, motivation, and character are also important, they contend, and for this reason many students, both white and minority, are rejected from selective colleges even though they receive top scores. In Bowen and Bok's opinion, schools should choose qualified applicants "who not only give promise of earning high grades but who also can enlarge the understanding of other students and contribute after graduation to their professions and communities." College affirmative action, they conclude, ensures a rich learning environment for all students and boosts the ranks of talented minority professionals.

Affirmative action is likely to provoke heated debate in the years to come. The following chapter explores various viewpoints on this controversial issue.

"Affirmative action has produced some tangible benefits for the nation as a whole."

Affirmative Action Has Furthered Civil Rights

Wilbert Jenkins

Since the 1960s, the U.S. government has used affirmative action to correct the effects of discrimination on women and minorities—typically by adopting policies that increase female and minority representation in the workforce. In the following viewpoint, Wilbert Jenkins explains that affirmative action policies are the outcome of civil rights laws designed to procure economic justice for African Americans. These policies have boosted the number of minorities attending college and entering the professional world, leading to the growth of the minority middle class. The author maintains, however, that recent rollbacks in affirmative action threaten this progress. Affirmative action must be retained to create a healthy and diverse workforce and to foster equal opportunity, he concludes. Jenkins is a history professor at Temple University in Philadelphia, Pennsylvania.

As you read, consider the following questions:
1. In what ways have whites been the recipients of preferential treatment, according to Jenkins?
2. In the author's opinion, what are the benefits of a diverse workforce?
3. In 1992, how much money did black men with bachelor's degrees earn in comparison to their white counterparts?

Excerpted from "Why We Must Retain Affirmative Action," by Wilbert Jenkins, *USA Today*, September 1999. Copyright © 1999 by the Society for the Advancement of Education.

The historical origins of affirmative action can be found in the 14th and 15th Amendments to the Constitution, the Enforcement Acts of 1870 and 1871, and the Civil Rights Acts of 1866 and 1875, which were passed by Republican-dominated Congresses during the Reconstruction period. This legislation set the precedent for many of the civil rights laws of the 1950s and 1960s—such as the Civil Rights Act of 1957, the Civil Rights Act of 1964, and the Voting Rights Act of 1965—and paved the way for what would become known as affirmative action.

In spite of the fact that laws designed to promote and protect the civil and political rights of African-Americans were enacted by Congress in the 1950s and 1960s, it was obvious that racism and discrimination against blacks in the area of education and, by extension, the workplace were huge obstacles that needed to be overcome if African-Americans were ever going to be able to carve an economic foundation. Thus, in the 1960s, affirmative action became a part of a larger design by Pres. Lyndon Johnson's War on Poverty program. In a historic 1965 speech at Howard University, the nation's top black school, Johnson illustrated the thinking that led to affirmative action: "You do not take a person who for years has been hobbled by chains and liberate him, bring him to the starting line and say you are free to compete with all the others." Civil rights leader Martin Luther King Jr. also underscored this belief when he stated that "one cannot ask people who don't have boots to pull themselves up by their own bootstraps."

Achieving Economic Justice

Policymakers fervently believed that more than three centuries of enslavement, oppression, and discrimination had so economically deprived African-Americans that some mechanism had to be put in place that would at least allow them a fighting chance. Blacks were locked out of the highest paid positions and made considerably fewer dollars than their white counterparts in the same jobs. Moreover, the number of African-Americans enrolling in the nation's undergraduate and graduate schools was extremely low. Affirmative action became a vehicle to correct this injustice. The original intent of affirmative action was not to provide jobs and other advantages to blacks solely because of the color of their skin, but to provide economic opportunities for those who are competent and qualified. Due to a history of discrimination, even those with outstanding credentials were often locked out. As the years wore on, it was deemed necessary to add other minorities—such as Native Americans, Hispanics, and Asian-Americans—as well as women to the list of those requiring affirmative action in order to achieve a measure of economic justice.

A number of conservatives—black and white—such as Armstrong Williams, Linda Chavez, Patrick Buchanan, Robert Novak, Ward Connerly, Clarence Thomas, Clint Bolick, Alan Keyes, and others argue that it is time to scrap affirmative action. This is necessary, they maintain, if the country is truly going to become a color-blind society like King envisioned. People would be judged by the content of their character, not by the color of their skin. Many among these conservatives also maintain that affirmative action is destructive to minorities because it is demeaning, saps drive, and leads to the development of a welfare dependency mentality. Minorities often come to believe that something is owed them.

Thus, conservatives argue against race-based admissions requirements to undergraduate and graduate schools, labeling them preferential treatment and an insult to anyone who is the beneficiary of this practice. In their opinion, it is psychologically, emotionally, and personally degrading for individuals to have to go through life realizing they were not admitted to school or given employment because of their credentials, but in order to fill some quota or to satisfy appearances. It is rather ironic, however, that they are so concerned about this apparent harm to black self-esteem, since there is little evidence that those who have been aided by affirmative action policies feel many doubts or misgivings. The vast majority of them believe they are entitled to whatever opportunities they have received—opportunities, in their estimation, which are long overdue because of racism and discrimination. Consequently, America is only providing them with a few economic crumbs which are rightfully theirs.

Countering Critics' Arguments

Although a number of affirmative action critics argue that lowering admissions standards for minorities creates a class of incompetent professionals—if they are somehow fortunate enough to graduate—the facts run counter to their arguments. For instance, a study conducted by Robert C. Davidson and Ernest L. Lewis of affirmative action students admitted to the University of California at Davis Medical School with low grades and test scores concluded that these students became doctors just as qualified as the higher-scoring applicants. The graduation rate of 94% for special-admissions students compared favorably to that of regular-admissions students (98%). Moreover, despite the fact that regular-admissions students were more likely to receive honors or A grades, there was no difference in the rates at which students failed core courses.

Many whites have been the recipients of some form of preferential treatment. For many years, so-called selective colleges have set less-demanding standards for admitting offspring of alumni or the children of the rich and famous. For example, though former Vice Pres. Dan Quayle's grade-point average was minuscule and his score on the LSAT very low, he was admitted to Indiana University's Law School. There is little evidence that Quayle or other recipients of this practice have developed low self-esteem or have felt any remorse for those whose credentials were better, but nonetheless were rejected because less-qualified others took their slots. The following example further underscores this practice. A number of opponents of affirmative action were embarrassed during 1996 in the midst of passage of Proposition 209, which eliminated affirmative action in California, when the *Los Angeles Times* broke a story documenting the fact that many of them and their children had received preferential treatment in acquiring certain jobs and gaining entry to some colleges.

Some opponents of affirmative action go so far as to suggest that it aggravates racial tensions and leads, in essence, to an increase in violence between whites and people of color. This simply does not mesh with historical reality. Discrimination against and violence toward the powerless always has increased during periods of economic downturns, as witnessed by the depressions of 1873 and 1893. There was nothing akin to affirmative action in this country for nearly two centuries of its existence, yet African-American women were physically and sexually assaulted by whites, and people of color were brutalized, murdered, and lynched on an unprecedented scale. Moreover, there were so many race riots in the summer of 1919 that the author of the black national anthem, James Weldon Johnson, referred to it as "the red summer." The 1920s witnessed the reemergence of a reinvigorated Ku Klux Klan. Many state politicians even went public with their memberships, and the governor of Indiana during this period was an avowed member of the Klan. The 1930s and 1940s did not bring much relief, as attested to by several race riots and Pres. Franklin D. Roosevelt's refusal to promote an anti-lynching bill.

Some of the African-American critics of affirmative action have actually been beneficiaries of such a program. It is unlikely that Clarence Thomas would have been able to attend Yale University Law School or become a justice on the U.S. Supreme Court without affirmative action. Yet, Thomas hates it with a passion, once saying he would be violating "God's law" if he ever signed his name to an opinion that approved the use of race—even for benign reasons—in hiring or admissions.

Whites Have Not Lost Ground

Opponents of affirmative action from various racial and ethnic backgrounds argue that it may lead to reverse discrimination, whereby qualified whites fail to acquire admission to school, secure employment, or are fired because of their race since prospective slots have to be preserved solely for minorities. It is difficult to say with any degree of certainty how many whites may have been bypassed or displaced because preferences have been given to blacks and other minorities. What can be said, though, with a large measure of accuracy is that whites have not lost ground in medicine and college teaching, despite considerable efforts to open up those fields. In addition, contrary to popular myth, there is little need for talented and successful advertising executives, lawyers, physicians, engineers, accountants, college professors, movie executives, chemists, physicists, airline pilots, architects, etc. to fear minority preference. Whites who lose out are more generally blue-collar workers or persons at lower administrative levels, whose skills are not greatly in demand.

Eleanor Mill. Reprinted by permission of Mill NewsArt Syndicate.

Furthermore, some whites who are passed over for promotion under these circumstances may simply not be viewed as the best person available for the job. It is human nature that those not receiving promotions that go to minorities or not gaining admission to colleges and universities prefer to believe that they have been discriminated against. They refuse to consider the possibility that the minorities could be better qualified. Although some highly qualified white students may be rejected by the University of California at Berkeley, Duke, Yale, Harvard, Stanford, or Princeton, the same students often are offered slots at Brown, Dartmouth, Cornell, Columbia, Michigan, the University of Pennsylvania, and the University of North Carolina at Chapel Hill— all first-rate institutions of higher learning. . . .

Tangible Benefits

Affirmative action has produced some tangible benefits for the nation as a whole. As a result of it, the number of minorities attending and receiving degrees from colleges and universities rose in the 1970s and 1980s. This led to an increase in the size of the African-American middle class. An attainment of higher levels of education, as well as affirmative action policies in hiring, helped blacks gain access to some professions that earlier had been virtually closed to them. For instance, it traditionally had been nearly impossible for African-Americans and other minorities to receive professorships at predominantly white schools. Some departments at these schools actively began to recruit and hire minority faculty as their campuses became more diverse.

As expected, African-American, Hispanic, Native American, and Asian-American students demanded that not only should more minority faculty be hired, but that the curriculum be expanded to include courses that deal with the cultural and historical experiences of their past. Some school administrators granted their demands, which has borne fruit in a number of ways. First, given the fact that the U.S. is steadily becoming even more multicultural, it is imperative that Americans learn about and develop an appreciation and respect for various cultures. This could enable those who plan to teach students from several different racial, cultural, and ethnic backgrounds in the public school system to approach their jobs with more sensitivity and understanding. Second, it is often crucial for minority faculty to act as role models, particularly on white campuses. Third, white students could profit by being taught by professors of color.

Since a white skin provides everyday advantages, having to face people of color in positions of authority may awaken some whites to realities about themselves and their society they previously have failed to recognize. It also might become obvious to them that certain racial stereotypes fly out of the window in light of intellectual exchanges with professors and peers of color.

Since education is crucial to acquiring economic advancement, it is of paramount importance that as many educational opportunities as possible be extended to the nation's minorities, which many studies indicate will total 50% of the population by 2050. Although much more is needed than affirmative action in order for minorities to gain the necessary access to higher levels of education and hiring, it nevertheless is the best mechanism to ensure at least a small measure of success in this regard. However, it currently is under attack in the areas of higher education, hiring, and Federal contracts. Now is the perfect time to find ways of improving affirmative action, rather than developing strategies aimed at destroying it. . . .

The Benefits of a Diverse Workforce

Many industries began downsizing in the late 1980s and the practice has continued in the 1990s, helping to reverse some of the earlier gains made by minorities. With American society steadily becoming even more multicultural, it makes good business sense to have a workforce that is reflective of this development. In order to make this a reality, affirmative action policies need to be kept in place, not abandoned. Why not use the expertise of African-Americans to target African-American audiences for business purposes or Asian-Americans to tap into potential Asian-American consumers? Businessmen who believe minorities will purchase products as readily from all-white companies as those which are perceived as diverse are seriously misguided.

A diverse workforce also can yield huge economic dividends in the international business sector, as became obvious in 1996 to Republicans who hoped to increase their majority in Congress and ride into the White House by attacking affirmative action policies in hiring. Rep. Dan Burton of Indiana, Speaker of the House Newt Gingrich, and presidential candidate Bob Dole, to name a few, applied pressure on businesses to end affirmative action policies in hiring. Executives informed them that this would be bad business and that the losses in revenue potentially would be staggering. In addition, it would be foolish public relations and substantially would reduce the pool of fine applicants. For the time being, the Republicans eased off.

A diverse workforce in a multicultural society makes practical and ethical sense. With all of the problems that need to be solved—such as disease, hunger, poverty, homelessness, lack of health care, racism, anti-Semitism, sexism, teenage pregnancy, crime, drugs, etc.—why should anyone's input be limited because of sex, race, color, class, or ethnic background? All Americans should be working together in this endeavor. It can best be accomplished by creating a truly diverse workforce through a continuation of affirmative action policies.

A Continuing Need

In spite of the fact that affirmative action has helped some African-Americans and other minorities achieve a middle-class status, not all have witnessed a significant improvement in their economic condition. For the most part, it has only helped the last generation of minorities. In order to make a significant impact, affirmative action policies need to be in place for several generations. Between 1970 and 1992, the median income for white families, computed in constant dollars, rose from $34,773 to $38,909, an increase of 11.9%. Black family income declined during this period, from $21,330 to $21,162. In relative terms, black incomes dropped from $613 to $544 for each $1,000 received by whites. Moreover, in 1992, black men with bachelor's degrees made $764 for each $1,000 received by white men with such degrees, and black males with master's degrees earned $870 for each $1,000 their white counterparts earned. Overall, black men received $721 for every $1,000 earned by white men.

Even more depressing for blacks is the fact that unemployment rates for them have remained at double-digit levels since 1975, averaging 14.9% for the 1980s, while the average was 6.3% for whites. The number of black children living below the poverty line reached 46.3% by 1992, compared to 12.3% of white children. At the same time, the overall poverty rate among Hispanics increased to 28.2%. Even in professions where blacks made breakthroughs by the early 1990s, they remained underrepresented. This was the case in engineering, law, medicine, dentistry, architecture, and higher education. Although blacks represented 10.2% of the workforce in 1992, they constituted just 3.7% of engineers, 2.7% of dentists, 3.1% of architects, and held 4.8% of university faculty positions.

Furthermore, while 27,713 doctoral degrees were awarded in 1992 to U.S. citizens and aliens who indicated their intention to remain in America, 1,081, or 3.9%, of these doctorates went to blacks. Given the low percentage of African-Americans receiving doctoral degrees, most college departments in all likelihood will find it difficult to recruit black faculty. With the hatchet steadily chopping affirmative action programs, this may become virtually impossible in the near future. The same holds true for other professions.

The most feasible way to ensure that colleges, universities, and various occupations will not become lily-white again is by the continuation of affirmative action. It gives minority groups that traditionally have been locked out of the education system and the workforce the best opportunity to carve out a solid economic foundation in America. I agree with Pres. Bill Clinton, who said, "Don't end it; mend it."

America has had over 200 years to deliver true justice, freedom, and equality to women and people of color. To believe that it now will make good the promise of equality without some kind of legislation to assist it is to engage in fantasy.

In advocating for affirmative action policies, people of color are not looking for government handouts. They merely are asking that some mechanism be kept in place to help provide the same social and economic opportunities most whites have had and continue to have access to.

*"Racial preferences designed to compensate
for prior discrimination are . . . inconsistent
with our most deeply cherished principles."*

Affirmative Action Has Hindered Civil Rights

Charles T. Canady

Prior to the mid-1960s, the civil rights movement fought
against racial discrimination by pushing for laws that emphasized color-blind principles of justice, contends Charles
T. Canady in the following viewpoint. But by the 1970s, so-
called affirmative action programs began using racial preferences in an attempt to ensure the proportional representation of minorities in the workforce. These programs are
discriminatory because they encourage employers to hire
people on the basis of race—with whites and members of
other nonpreferred groups frequently being denied job opportunities. Furthermore, Canady charges, affirmative action preferences lead both whites and nonwhites to doubt
minority competence. Such preferences undermine the original goals of the civil rights movement, Canady maintains.
Canady is a Republican representative from Florida.

As you read, consider the following questions:
1. What were Jim Crow laws, according to Canady?
2. What famous U.S. document sets forth the ideal of
   individual dignity, according to the author?
3. In Canady's opinion, how would black disadvantage best
   be addressed?

Excerpted from "America's Struggle for Racial Equity," by Charles T. Canady,
Policy Review, January/February 1998. Reprinted with permission from *Policy
Review*.

On June 11, 1963, in the wake of Governor George Wallace's stand against integration at the University of Alabama, President John F. Kennedy reported to the American people on the state of civil rights in the nation. He called on Congress to pass legislation dismantling the system of segregation and encouraged lawmakers to make a commitment "to the proposition that race has no place in American life or law."

Invoking the equality of all Americans before the law, Kennedy said: "We are confronted primarily with a moral issue. It is as old as the Scriptures and it is as clear as the American Constitution. The heart of the question is whether all Americans are to be afforded equal rights and equal opportunities, whether we are going to treat our fellow Americans as we want to be treated."

The American people are now beginning a great debate over the use of race and gender preferences by federal, state, and local governments. In 1996, a majority of voters in California, including 29 percent of blacks, approved the California Civil Rights Initiative prohibiting preferential treatment in public employment, education, and contracting. In a series of cases, the Supreme Court and federal courts of appeal have made it clear that the system of preference is built on an exceedingly shaky foundation. These cases—chiefly the *Adarand* decision of 1995—establish that racial classifications are presumptively unconstitutional and will be permitted only in extraordinary circumstances. In [the future], Congress is likely to consider legislation to end the use of race and gender preferences by the federal government.

Unequal Treatment

As we enter this debate, Kennedy's stirring words on civil rights are as important as they were in 1963. In the name of overcoming discrimination, our government for the past generation has been treating Americans of different races unequally. This is not the first time that American governments have intentionally discriminated. The institution of slavery and Jim Crow laws both violated the fundamental American tenet that "all men are created equal" and are "endowed by their Creator with certain unalienable rights." But racial preferences designed to compensate for prior discrimination are also inconsistent with our most deeply cherished principles.

Slavery was the single greatest injustice in American history. The conflict sparked by its existence and by efforts to expand it took 365,000 American lives. A system of ferocious violence that degraded human beings to the status of chattel, American slavery had at its core the belief that blacks were subhuman. It was an institution that systematically and wantonly trampled on the most basic of human relations: Husband was separated from wife, parent was separated from child. Liberty was denied to individuals solely by reason of race.

When this disgraceful chapter in our history came to an end, it left a legacy of racism that has afflicted America up to the present generation. Soon after the Civil War, that legacy found expression in the segregation statutes, also known as Jim Crow laws. Historian C. Vann Woodward describes segregation thus: "That code lent the sanction of law to a social ostracism that extended to churches and schools, to housing and jobs, to eating and drinking. Whether by law or by custom, that ostracism extended to virtually all forms of public transportation, to sports and recreations, to hospitals, orphanages, prisons, and asylums, and ultimately to funeral homes, morgues, and cemeteries."

Woodward continues, "The Jim Crow laws, unlike feudal laws, did not assign the subordinated group a fixed status in society. They were constantly pushing the Negro farther down." Woodward also documents the "total disfranchisement" of black voters in the South through the poll tax and the white primary. He quotes Edgar Gardner Murphy on the attitude of many southern whites that energized the system of segregation during the first half of the 20th century: "Its spirit is that of an all-absorbing autocracy of race, an animus of aggrandizement which makes, in the imagination of the white man, an absolute identification of the stronger race with the being of the state."

A Question of Dignity

The civil-rights movement of the 1950s and the early 1960s arose to combat racist laws, racist institutions, and racist practices wherever they existed. The story of that movement is a glorious chapter in the history of America. Sparked by the Supreme Court's decision in *Brown v. Board of Education* (1954), the civil rights movement dealt a death blow to the system of segregation with the passage of the Civil Rights Act of 1964. The Voting Rights Act of 1965 soon followed, creating the basis for fully restoring the franchise to black Americans throughout the country.

The moral example of those who stood against the forces of racial injustice played a critical role in reshaping American attitudes toward race. The American people were moved by images of the terrible acts of violence and gross indignities visited on black Americans.

Moreover, the civil-rights movement embodied a fundamental message that touched the soul of the American people. It exemplified an ideal at the core of the American experience from the very beginning of our national life, an ideal that was never fully realized and sometimes tragically perverted, but always acknowledged by Americans.

The ideal of respect for the dignity of the individual was set forth in the Declaration of Independence: "[A]ll men are created equal" and are "endowed by their Creator with certain unalienable rights." At Independence Hall on the eve of the Civil War, Lincoln spoke of this ideal as "a great principle or idea" in the Declaration of Independence "which gave promise that in due time the weights should be lifted from the shoulders of all men, and that all should have an equal chance." This ideal undergirded the civil-rights movement and condemned the contradictions of America's segregated society. . . .

An Animating Principle

This understanding of the dignity of the individual found concrete expression in a legal principle that was relentlessly pursued by the early civil-rights movement. If universally adopted, this principle would fulfill the promise of American ideals. It was eloquently stated by the first Justice Harlan in his dissent to the Supreme Court's decision in *Plessy v. Ferguson* (1896). In words that would often be cited by those seeking to overthrow the odious Jim Crow system, Harlan pronounced, "Our Constitution is color blind. . . . The law regards man as man, and takes no account of his surroundings or of his color when his civil rights as guaranteed by the Supreme law of the land are involved."

The colorblind principle articulated by Harlan was the touchstone of the American civil-rights movement until the mid-1960s. Emory law professor Andrew Kull, in his admirable history *The Color-Blind Constitution*, identifies the centrality of the colorblind principle to the movement: "The undeniable fact is that over a period of some 125 years ending only in the late 1960s, the American civil-rights movement first elaborated, then held as its unvarying political objective, a rule of law requiring the color-blind treatment of individuals.". . .

The principle of colorblind justice ultimately did find clear expression in the law of the United States. By passing the Civil Rights Act of 1964, Congress acted decisively against the Jim Crow system, and established a national policy against discrimination based on race and sex. It is the supreme irony of the modern civil-rights movement that this crowning achievement was soon followed by the creation of a system of preferences based first on race and then extended to gender.

The Civil Rights Act of 1964 was an unequivocal statement that Americans should be treated as individuals and not as members of racial and gender groups. Congress rejected the racism of America's past. Under the Civil Rights Act of 1964, no American would be subject to discrimination. And there was no question about what discrimination meant. Senator Hubert Humphrey of Minnesota—the chief Senate sponsor of the legislation—stated it as clearly as possible: Discrimination was any "distinction in treatment given to different individuals because of their different race."

Was This Enough?

As the Civil Rights Act was being considered, some voices questioned the adequacy of the principle of colorblind justice. The Urban League's Whitney Young said that "300 years of deprivation" called for "a decade of discrimination in favor of Negro youth." James Farmer, a founder of the Congress of Racial Equality, called for "compensatory preferential treatment." Farmer said "it was impossible" for an "employer to be oblivious to color because we had all grown up in a racist society." But Roy Wilkins of the National Association for the Advancement of Colored People, in an encounter with Farmer, summed up the traditional view of the civil-rights movement: "I have a problem with that whole concept. What you're asking for there is not equal treatment, but special treatment to make up for the unequal treatment of the past. I think that's outside the American tradition and the country won't buy it. I don't feel at all comfortable asking for any special treatment; I just want to be treated like everyone else."

While considering the Civil Rights Act of 1964, Congress itself debated the issues of racial preferences and proportional representation. The result of that debate was the adoption of Section 703(j) of the Act, which states that nothing in Title VII of the Act "shall be interpreted to require any employer . . . to grant preferential treatment to any individual or group because of the race . . . of such individual or group" in order to maintain a racial balance. Senators Joseph Clark of Pennsylvania and Clifford Case of New Jersey, who steered that section of Title VII through the legislative process, left no doubt about Congress's intent. "[A]ny deliberate attempt to maintain a racial balance," they said at the time, "whatever such a balance may be, would involve a violation of Title VII because maintaining such a balance would require an employer to hire or refuse to hire on the basis of race. It must be emphasized that discrimination is prohibited to any individual."

Led Astray

For a brief, shining moment, the principle of colorblind justice was recognized as the law of the land. But soon that principle was thrust aside to make way for a system of race-based entitlement. The critical events took place during the Nixon administration, when the so-called Philadelphia Plan was adopted. It became the prototypical program of racial preferences for federal contractors.

In February 1970, the U.S. Department of Labor issued an order that the affirmative-action programs adopted by all government contractors must include "goals and timetables to which the contractor's good faith efforts must be directed to correct . . . deficiencies" in the "utilization of minority groups." This construct of goals and timetables to ensure the proper utilization of minority groups clearly envisioned a system of proportional representation in which group identity would be a factor—often the decisive factor—in hiring decisions. Embodied in this bureaucratic verbiage was a policy requiring that distinctions in treatment be made on the basis of race.

Henry Payne. Reprinted with permission from United Media.

Discrimination of a most flagrant kind is now practiced at the federal, state, and local levels. A white teacher in Piscataway, New Jersey, is fired solely on account of her race. Asian students are denied admission to state universities to make room for students of other races with much weaker records. There are more than 160 federal laws, regulations, and executive orders explicitly requiring race- and sex-based preferences.

Now, as throughout the history of preferences, the key issue in the debate is how policies of preference can be reconciled with the fundamental American tenet that "all men are created equal" and are "endowed by their Creator with certain unalienable rights."

Evidence of racism can still be found in our country. American society is not yet colorblind. The issue for Americans today is how we can best transcend the divisions of the past. Is it through a policy of consistent nondiscrimination or through a system of preferences?

Racial preferences are frequently justified as a measure to help low-income blacks. But the evidence is compelling that the beneficiaries of preferential policies are overwhelmingly middle-class or wealthy. For the most part, the truly disadvantaged have been unable to participate in the programs that grant preferences. Furthermore, the emphasis on preferences has diverted attention from the task of addressing the root causes of black Americans' disadvantage. The lagging educational achievement of disadvantaged blacks can be ameliorated not through preferences but through structural reform of the American elementary and secondary education system. Preferences do nothing to help develop the skills necessary for the economic and social advancement of the disadvantaged.

Dressed-Up Discrimination

Preferences must also be judged a moral failure. Although some individuals have benefited significantly from preferences and a case can be made that preferences have enhanced the economic position of the black middle class, these gains have come at a great moral cost. Put simply, preferences discriminate. They deny opportunities to individuals solely because they are members of a nonpreferred race, gender, or ethnic group. The ambitions and aspirations, the hopes and dreams of individual Americans for themselves and for their families are trampled underfoot not for any wrongs those individuals have committed but for the sake of a bureaucratic effort to counterbalance the supposedly pervasive racism of American society. The penalty for the sins of the society at large is imposed on individuals who themselves are guilty only of being born a member of a nonpreferred group. Individual American citizens who would otherwise enjoy jobs and other opportunities are told that they must be denied in order to tilt the scales of racial justice.

Although preferences are presented as a remedial measure, they in fact create a class of innocent victims of government-imposed discrimination. In our system of justice, the burden of a remedy is imposed on those responsible for the specific harm being remedied. In the case of racial preferences, however, this remedial model breaks down. Those who benefit from the remedy need not show that they have in fact suffered any harm, and those who bear the burden of the remedy do so not because of any conduct on their part but purely because of their identity as members of non-preferred groups. Americans of all descriptions are deprived of opportunities under the system of preferences. And some of these victims have themselves struggled to overcome a severely disadvantaged background.

The proponents of preferential policies must acknowledge the injuries done to innocent individuals. They must confront the consequences flowing daily from the system of preferences in awarding contracts, jobs, promotions, and other opportunities. Supporters of the status quo attempt to hide the reality of preferences beneath a facade of "plus factors," "goals and timetables," and other measures that are said merely to "open up access" to opportunities. Behind all these semantic games, individual Americans are denied opportunities by government simply because they are of the wrong color or sex. The names assigned to the policies that deprive them of opportunity are of little moment. What matters is that our government implements a wide range of programs with the purpose of granting favored treatment to some on the basis of their biological characteristics. How can such government-imposed distinctions be reconciled with Martin Luther King's message that whenever the image of God is recognized as universally present in mankind, "'whiteness' and 'blackness' pass away as determinants in a relationship"? The conflict is irreconcilable.

The moral failure of preferences extends beyond the injustice done to individuals who are denied opportunities because they belong to the wrong group. There are other victims of the system of preferences. The supposed beneficiaries are themselves victims.

Preferences attack the dignity of the preferred, and cast a pall of doubt over their competence and worth. Preferences send a message that those in the favored groups are deemed incapable of meeting the standards that others are required to meet. Simply because they are members of a preferred group, individuals are often deprived of the recognition and respect they have earned. The achievements gained through talent and hard work are attributed instead to the operation of the system of preferences. The abilities of the preferred are called into question not only in the eyes of society, but also in the eyes of the preferred themselves. Self-confidence erodes, standards drop, incentives to perform diminish, and pernicious stereotypes are reinforced.

All of this results from treating individuals differently on the basis of race. It is the inevitable consequence of reducing individuals to the status of racial entities. The lesson of our history as Americans is that racial distinctions are inherently cruel. There are no benign distinctions of race. Our history—and perhaps human nature itself—renders that impossible. Although the underlying purpose of preferences was to eliminate the vestiges of racism, the mechanism of redress was fundamentally flawed. Rather than breaking down racial barriers, preferential policies continually remind Americans of racial differences.

"[Affirmative action] initiatives produce concrete educational benefits for white as well as minority students."

Affirmative Action in Admissions Benefits College Students

Martin Michaelson

Affirmative action policies benefit all college students, contends Martin Michaelson in the following viewpoint. The consideration of race and ethnicity in admissions has had a negligible effect on white student attendance, Michaelson points out. In the meantime, affirmative action brings a healthy racial diversity to college campuses—a diversity that enhances students' personal and academic development. Moreover, the author asserts, college affirmative action programs have fostered a growing middle class of successful minority professionals. Michaelson, a Washington, D.C.-based attorney, represents colleges and universities throughout the United States.

As you read, consider the following questions:
1. Why are there such strong objections to the use of affirmative action in college admissions decisions, in Michaelson's opinion?
2. According to the author, what is problematic about the concept of "merit?"
3. In Michaelson's view, why will colleges and universities be the "emergency rooms of the 21st century?"

Reprinted from "Affirmative Action in College and University Admissions: Yes," by Martin Michaelson, *National Forum: The Phi Kappa Phi Journal*, vol. 79, no. 1, Winter 1999. Copyright © 1999 by Martin Michaelson. Reprinted with permission from *National Forum: The Phi Kappa Phi Journal*.

As a journeyman lawyer, who on a good day sits at the feet of the likes of Derek Bok, William Bowen, and Ronald Dworkin, I perhaps have no business addressing here the question of why affirmative action in admissions is sound policy. *The Shape of the River: Long-term Consequences of Considering Race in College and University Admissions*, Bowen and Bok's analysis, is empirical and erudite. Dworkin's essays in *The New York Review of Books* ("Affirming Affirmative Action," October 22, 1998; "Is Affirmative Action Doomed?" November 5, 1998) meticulously appraise the arguments and pertinent jurisprudence. These works go far toward remedying the long-felt need for stronger scholarship in this touchy field.

Until these and a handful of other carefully reasoned publications came forward, few issues under broad public discussion were characterized by a less illuminating ratio of heat to light than this one. Strident polemic drowned out more thoughtful voices.

Several reasons seem plain. A college degree has become for most Americans, perhaps to an unprecedented extent, the *sine qua non* of upward economic mobility. Census data show the surprisingly large amount by which average annual incomes of bachelors-degree holders exceed incomes even of those who attended college but did not graduate. Competition for admission to the most prestigious colleges, many of whose graduates occupy envied positions, has grown more rivalrous. Rejection from these top institutions can be painful, not least to parents who want the world for their children. No great imagination is needed to see why blacks and other minorities are blamed when moderately well-qualified white daughters and sons are denied entry to the élite college that is their first choice. Also, statements of federal officials during the Reagan and Bush administrations—as well as litigation brought by conservative groups, Proposition 209 in California, Initiative 200 in Washington State, legislation proposed in Congress, and other political developments—have contributed to the impression that white students are being unjustly barred from college.

Yet the noise this issue generates should not, as a factual

matter, be mainly attributable to exclusion of white applicants. True, the most selective institutions were virtually lily-white until the 1950s, and no longer are. Harvard's dormitories were effectively segregated until World War II, and the private college that was most integrated before 1950 (Oberlin, which had a practice of race sensitivity dating to the Underground Railroad) found itself unable to sustain a four percent participation rate for blacks. But affirmative action in the 1970s, 1980s, and 1990s has hardly turned the institutions upside down. Even at the twenty-eight top-tier colleges and universities whose racial demographics Bowen and Bok studied, the foreclosure—if that is the right word—attributable to affirmative action is a small fraction of enrollments. Most college students today, as in prior years, attend institutions where all or nearly all qualified applicants are admitted and where race and ethnicity do not figure in admissions decisions.

Further, those selective colleges and universities that do take into account the race and ethnicity of historically underrepresented minority applicants ordinarily assign greater and more dispositive weight to all applicants' scores, grades, and extracurricular achievements. The effect, in statistical terms, of race- and ethnicity-targeted admissions policies on the probability that a prototypical white applicant will not be admitted to one of these selective institutions is virtually negligible. Elimination of the programs would increase the white applicant's probability of admission, which is about 25 percent, only to about 26.5 percent, according to extensive data available to Bowen and Bok.

Is this, then, really a debate about opportunity? By numerous measurements, opportunity for white persons in the United States today far exceeds that for blacks, Hispanics, and Native Americans. The gaping disparity between college graduation rates of whites and members of those groups has been increasing, not decreasing, and is projected to widen, not narrow. Whites continue to make much more money on average than do those minorities. Whites still occupy federal, state, and local public office in disproportion to their numbers. And whites dominate, also disproportionately, every profession and occupation accorded status, except professional sports (where whites control management) and, to the extent so regarded, the enlisted military ranks. There is no serious argument that affirmative-action programs of the limited type now administered by the institutions of higher education that have them will reverse white domination in our lifetimes, if ever.

Why the Outcry?

If the effects of these programs on whites are in fact relatively slight, as they appear to be, and if those effects do not threaten the preponderant authority of whites in a society where that always has been basic, what accounts for so much outcry by opponents of these temperate policies? One possible answer is that the programs offer a case study for some in the majority to claim rhetorically, after all these years, the moral high ground in a matter of race. It is not easy for whites in America to find a pretext for victimization; here one is. The programs supply some minority group members a case study as well. Here they can propound a different rhetoric, in which *their* victimization is traced to social engineering by a patronizing white intellectual aristocracy. Nor should we gainsay the rhetorical excesses of some affirmative action advocates.

Much of the rhetoric of the argument over affirmative action in admissions is simplistic, inflammatory, and unsatisfying. Shall university policies be "color-blind" or "race-conscious"? Do we favor "merit" or "preferences"? These and similar buzzwords, in the context of this issue, have no self-evident, commonly shared, or full definition.

Thus, for example, proponents of "color blindness" surely do not mean that in the conduct of day-to-day affairs we are or have practicable means to become oblivious to the race and ethnicity of all persons with whom we have contact. Nor can thoughtful supporters of an exclusive attention to "merit" seriously believe that any person's qualifications are fully expressed in a standardized test score, high school grades, and musical, athletic, or other skill; our merit as human beings is of course to some degree informed by how well we have played the hand life dealt us, how far we have come. Also, to be meaningful, merit must conduce to its object. If diversity of the student body is a legitimate interest of a college—a proposition against which few today contend—then an applicant's advancement of that interest must be at least germane to merit for admission. (How odd it would be for a college to recruit for geographic, cultural, religious, and other student diversity, yet omit race and ethnicity, forms of diversity emblematic of both our nation's highest aspirations and its toughest problems.) The rhetoric of the higher-education affirmative-action controversy, in short, does not help us determine whether the concept is sound.

Choosing Who Gets Admitted

There's almost no responsible person in education, or no well-regarded educator, who thinks that it would be sound public policy to admit people to a school simply on the basis of grades and test scores. The reason that would be irresponsible public policy is because it wouldn't create the kind of setting that facilitates education. It wouldn't create diversity—not just ethnic diversity but diversity of a number of lines. Furthermore, it wouldn't be any more efficient a way to choose people who get educated. Once you're above a certain benchmark score, let's say, on the SAT test or have a certain benchmark level of grades in high school, if we're talking about college admission, you can do the work. You're qualified to go to college, and you're going to perform successfully there.

The affirmative-action issue arises when we look at all these people who are qualified to be educated at Harvard Law School, or the University of Maryland, or wherever. Then we ask, "Among all these people who are qualified, how do we choose who gets admitted?" Ironically, even in the few jurisdictions that have passed anti-affirmative-action laws, the law in those jurisdictions is that it's perfectly fine to consider where they were born, or whether their fathers give a lot of money to the school, or whether they played sports. But you just can't consider race.

Paul Butler, *World & I*, September 1998.

Nor is the issue resolved by reference to the particulars of this or that university's affirmative-action program. The possibility that an excellent idea may be applied somewhere in a non-excellent way is no more remarkable in this context than in any other. In this respect, the contentions of some opponents of the diversity-promoting efforts can be analogized to a claim that democracy is no good because unqualified citizens are sometimes elected to office, or the religion is evil because some evangelical preachers on television are mendacious.

The Legal Record

In a nation not only of laws but also, to say the least, of lawyers, we habitually look to the law to inform us whether a policy is wise. But in matters involving racial and ethnic inclusion our law has been an unreliable teacher. Consider, for example, two famous decisions, rendered in 1896 and 1996. The first, *Plessy v. Ferguson*, a ruling by a nearly unanimous Supreme Court two generations after the Civil War, held that the Constitution authorizes wholesale exclusion of blacks from public accommodations occupied by whites. (In the education field, the durable results of *Plessy's* "separate but equal" doctrine persisted long after the high court's contrary rule, fifty-eighty years later, in *Brown v. Board of Education*.) The 1996 decision *University of Texas v. Hopwood*, from the Fifth Circuit Court of Appeals, held that colleges and universities in Texas, Louisiana, and Mississippi, in attempting to assemble diverse student bodies, are entirely forbidden to consider applicants' race and ethnicity. Two of the three judges who ruled in the case went so far as to assert that race and ethnicity are no more relevant than a student's blood type.

To date, only one Supreme Court decision has addressed affirmative action in admissions, *Regents of the University of California v. Bakke* (1978). Unable to agree on a rationale, the nine Justices issued six opinions in the case. The lead opinion, by Justice Lewis F. Powell Jr., held that admission quotas for racial or ethnic groups are unconstitutional, but that race and ethnicity may lawfully be considered as one factor among the many that may pertain to an applicant's suitability for admission. Justice Powell emphasized the importance of university autonomy in academic decision-making, a right grounded in the First Amendment.

However, many observers now question whether, in light of the rightward leanings of today's Supreme Court, the

Bakke principle will be upheld when the issue is re-examined by the Justices, which could happen within a few years. We simply do not know whether the Court's next pronouncement will endorse *Bakke*'s balanced doctrine, or whether, as with *Plessy v. Ferguson*, posterity will judge the Court's next statement a disgrace.

What *do* we know with any confidence about the value of affirmative action in admissions? Putting aside the empty rhetoric, and doubting the judgment of judges, and discounting, as we should, arguments founded on unrepresentative facts and hyperbole, where can we turn for insight?

Informative Evidence

The most informative evidence available is from the actual experience of colleges and universities with such programs. Although not yet fully marshaled, that evidence strongly supports diversity-enhancing practices that to a limited extent take race and ethnicity into account. Studies that address recruitment of a racially diverse student body have found that the initiatives produce concrete educational benefits for white as well as minority students.

For example, Professor Alexander Astin surveyed 25,000 students in 217 four-year colleges, assessing attitudes, values, beliefs, career plans, achievement, and degree completion. He found that emphasis on diversity is associated with "widespread beneficial effects on a student's cognitive and affective development." "[T]he weight of the empirical evidence," he concluded, "shows that the actual effects on student development of emphasizing diversity and of student participation in diversity activities are overwhelmingly positive." Professor Astin's research also shows that students who interact more with students of different backgrounds tend to be more successful in college, and that students' direct experiences with diversity are positively associated with many measures of academic development and achievement.

In *The Shape of the River*, William Bowen and Derek Bok analyze data on more than 80,000 students who entered eleven colleges and seventeen universities in 1951, 1976, and 1989, 45,000 of them in the latter two years. The data are eye-opening. To cite one example: Among approximately

700 blacks who matriculated at the schools in 1976, but who likely would have been denied admission under entirely race-neutral admissions policies, more than 225 attained professional degrees or doctorates; nearly 125 are business executives; and over 300 are active in civic life. The data led Bowen and Bok to observe that "[o]n inspection, many of the arguments against considering race in admissions—such as allegations of unintended harm to the intended beneficiaries and enhanced racial tensions on campus—seem to us to lack substance."

The Shape of the River demonstrates nothing less than that affirmative action in admissions has fostered an emerging black middle class increasingly prepared for the American mainstream. "Let us suppose," say Bowen and Bok, "that rejecting, on race-neutral grounds, more than half of the black students who otherwise would attend these institutions would raise the probability of acceptance for another white student from 25 to, say, 27 percent at the most selective colleges and universities. Would we, as a society, be better off? Considering both the educational benefits of diversity and the need to include far larger numbers of black graduates in the top ranks of the business, professional, governmental, and not-for-profit institutions that shape our society we do not think so."

No Feasible Alternative

Often it is asserted that the benefits of student diversity could be achieved in a less controversial way, such as by recruiting low-income applicants or those from other population sub-sets that may coincidentally correlate with minority groups. Substantial hard evidence, however, including studies by Professor Thomas Kane of Harvard, shows otherwise. No feasible alternative to race- and ethnicity-targeted efforts has yet been found.

We are not a mean-spirited people for arguing about who should be invited to sit in the limited number of chairs at the best colleges and universities, although the controversy has been no model of reasoned discourse. Underlying the disagreements is a shared belief that the quality of our lives will depend more than ever before on the quality of higher education. During the lifetimes of today's high school students, racial and ethnic groups now in the minority will be half of America's population. (In the coming decade alone, there will be some two million more black and Hispanic eighteen-to twenty-four-year-olds than at present.) If a calamitous state of public affairs is to be averted, members of these severely underrepresented groups must be admitted in substantial numbers to the excellent institutions of higher education long accessible only to whites. In relation to this nation's well-being, colleges and universities will be the emergency rooms of the 21st century. Let us at least agree that this is an exceptionally dangerous time for them to turn away the historically underserved.

| "*Preferential affirmative action on our campus . . . has driven race relations among us to a point lower than it has ever been.*"

Affirmative Action in Admissions Harms College Students

Carl Cohen

The original intention of affirmative action—the elimination of racially discriminatory practices—is honorable, Carl Cohen maintains in the following viewpoint. He contends, however, that the racial preferences that have arisen in the name of affirmative action are unfair and intolerable. This is especially noticeable on college campuses, Cohen argues, where the favoritism toward minorities in admissions policies has placed costly burdens on student populations. Preferred minorities are stigmatized because they are seen as needing special treatment to succeed, resulting in the humiliation of minority students and resentment among white students. Cohen is a philosophy professor at the University of Michigan and has served on that university's admissions committees.

As you read, consider the following questions:
1. According to Cohen, when were racial preferences introduced?
2. In the words of Justice Lewis Powell, cited by the author, what kind of diversity should universities seek?
3. What four large groups have to bear the burdens of racial preferences, in Cohen's opinion?

Excerpted from "Race Preference in College Admissions," by Carl Cohen, *Heritage Lectures, no. 611*, April 29, 1998. Reprinted with permission from the Heritage Foundation.

"Affirmative action" has long had many meanings. The Civil Rights Act of 1964 authorized courts to take "affirmative action" to uproot racially discriminatory practices. That objective was, and remains, morally right. But that same statute forbade race preference; it is morally wrong. Affirmative action and race preference are thus plainly distinguishable; the former (in its original sense) is right and lawful, the latter is neither.

Preference and affirmative action are widely confounded in the public mind because race preferences were introduced (beginning about 1970) in the honorable name of affirmative action. What was to have been eliminated was given the name of what had been designed to eliminate it. Most folks today, with unintended irony, mean by "affirmative action" that very preference by skin color that affirmative action was devised to eradicate.

The result is doubly unfortunate: Wrongful practices fly the flag of justice, and morally right policies are smeared by association with what everyone sees intuitively to be unfair. Remedy for identifiable injuries inflicted by a given institution is a demand of justice; but that is redress for damage from that institution, not preference by color. Henceforth, let us be clear: It is not affirmative action but generalized race preference that is at issue. That our universities do give systematic preference by skin color—often blatantly—is indisputable. . . . we all know that it is so.

Race Preference Is Wrong

Here is the fundamental principle: Giving preference by race, by skin color, is wrong, unjust; when done by an agency of the state it is unlawful, a violation of federal statutes and of our Constitution. The motives are often good; we understand that. But the conduct is wrong and not tolerable in a good society.

I begin with this historical note: In his Brief in the case of *Brown v. Board of Education*, Thurgood Marshall, then executive director of the Legal Defense Fund of the National Association for the Advancement of Colored People, wrote in 1954: "Distinctions by race are so evil, so arbitrary and invidious that a state, bound to defend the equal protection of the laws must not invoke them in any public sphere."

I cheered when I read that then, as I cheer today when I re-read it. The truth of this principle does not change with the times. Let us seek to respond justly to injury, giving appropriate remedy where remedy is due, and credit where credit is due, without regard to race. But if ever we are to heal our racial wounds it will be through a national determination, morally resolute and backed by law where that is appropriate, never again to give preference by race or color or sex. The long-term success of a democratic polity requires a deep and widespread commitment to the principle that the laws protect all equally.

Racial discrimination is wrong, no matter the color preferred. We begin to transcend racism when we stop the practice of every form of it, by every public body, now. To give favor to males or to females, or to whites or to blacks or to persons of any color, is morally wrong because doing so is intrinsically unfair. Color, nationality, and sex are not attributes that entitle anyone to more (or less) of the good things in life, or to any special favor (or disfavor). When, in the past, whites or males did receive such preference that was deeply wrong; it is no less wrong now when the colors or sexes are reversed. Justice Marshall long ago made it clear that the plain words of federal law "proscribe racial discrimination . . . against whites on the same terms as racial discrimination against non-whites."

Equality applies to all.

Only Individuals Possess Rights

But what of those who have been badly hurt by earlier racial discrimination? Do they not deserve to be compensated? Yes, of course; persons may indeed be entitled to remedy for unlawful injury done to them because they were black or brown or female. We give such remedy, rightly—but it is the injury for which remedy is given, not the skin color or sex. There is all the difference in the world between compensation for injury and preference by race.

When preference is given flatly by skin color or by national origin, the inevitable result is the award of advantages to some who deserve no advantage, and the imposition of burdens upon some who deserve no burden. Most often, those who benefit did not suffer the wrong for which compensation is supposedly being given; those who are disadvantaged by the preference most often did not do any wrong whatsoever, and certainly not that earlier wrong to a minority group for which the preference is alleged redress.

The oppression of blacks and some other minorities in our country has been grievous, a stain on our history; no honest person will deny that. But the notion that we can redress that historical grievance by giving preference now to persons in the same racial or sexual group as those earlier wronged is a mistake, a blunder. It supposes that rights are possessed by groups, and that therefore advantages given to some minority group now can be payment for earlier injuries to other members of that minority. But moral entitlements are not held by groups. Whites as a group do not have rights, and blacks as a group do not have rights; rights are possessed by persons, individual human persons. And when persons are entitled to be made whole for some injury earlier done to them, the duty owed is not to members of their race or sex or nationality, not to their group, but to them as individuals. The effort to defend preference as group compensation fails because it fundamentally misconceives the relation between wrongs and remedies.

This does not mean that affirmative action must be abandoned. In its original sense, affirmative action was intended to insure the elimination of racially discriminatory practices, and no reasonable person would want to oppose that. But if by affirmative action one means (as many Americans now do mean) preferential devices designed to bring about redistribution of the good things in life to match ethnic proportions in the population, affirmative action in that sense must be rejected because the preferences it employs are inconsistent with the equal treatment of all persons.

A Misrepresentation of Diversity

The argument applies to our public universities with special force, because here the habits of democracy are molded. But many universities now give very marked preference by race and seek to justify what they do by the quest for diversity. A diverse student body is an appropriate goal for a university—but that goal, as Justice Lewis F. Powell said explicitly in his opinion in *University of California v. Bakke*, is intellectual diversity, diversity of judgment and viewpoint. When our universities announce that they are striving for diversity, we know that what they are really seeking to achieve is racial proportionality; they profess an intellectual objective, but their real goal is racial balance. This passion for racial balance "misconceives"—that is Justice Powell's word—the diversity that might serve educative ends. And however meritorious those educative ends, it is worth noting that they cannot possibly serve as the "compelling" objective that is required for the constitutional use of racial classifications by the state.

Justice Powell, in *Bakke*, very specifically addressed this "racial balance" defense of admissions preference; he wrote that such a purpose is "facially invalid," invalid on its face! He concludes: "Preferring members of any one group for no reason other than race or ethnic origin is discrimination for its own sake. This the Constitution forbids."

This principle of equal treatment is the moral foundation upon which the Equal Protection Clause of the 14th Amendment ultimately rests; our Supreme Court has repeatedly emphasized that the rights guaranteed by that clause are individual rights, the rights of persons ["No state shall . . . deny to any person the equal protection of the laws"] and not the rights of groups. Race preferences in admission fly in the face of the Civil Rights Act of 1964, whose Section 603 reads, in full:

> No person in the United States shall, on the ground of race, color, or national origin, be excluded from participation in, be denied the benefits of, or be subjected to discrimination under any program or activity receiving Federal financial assistance.

And race preferences fly in the face of the Equal Protection Clause. Justice Powell, in *Bakke*, put this eloquently:

> The guarantee of equal protection cannot mean one thing when applied to one individual and something else when applied to a person of another color. If both are not accorded the same protection, then it is not equal.

That is why every program relying upon naked preference by race or sex, whether in the form of set-asides in the award of contracts or bonuses for hiring persons of certain colors, or additional consideration in competitive employment, or college admissions—all such preferences, whether defended as compensatory or as redistributive, or for the sake of racial diversity—must be unjust.

The Burdens of Race Preference

Beyond its unfairness, racial preference is injurious and counterproductive. Ask yourself: Who reaps the benefits and who bears the burdens of race preference?

The beneficiaries of race preference are a few members of the preferred group (if, in fact, they succeed in graduating from the college to which they have been preferentially admitted), and the newly emerged corps of administrators whose livelihood is derived from the oversight and enforcement of preferences. The vast majority of the members of the minority groups in question—in whose interests preferences had purportedly been designed—receive no benefits whatever.

The burdens of preference, on the other hand, are borne by four large groups, for each of which the costs are greater by far than the alleged returns.

1. The cruelest burdens, the most damaging and the longest-lasting, are those borne by the members of the preferred minority group as a whole, who are inescapably undermined by racial preferences. When persons are appointed, admitted, or promoted because of their racial group, it is inevitable that the members of that group will, in the institution giving such preference, perform less well on average. Membership in the minority group most certainly does not imply inferiority; that is a canard—but that stereotype is reinforced by the preferences given.

Since the standards for the selection of minorities are, by hypothesis, lower, because they were diluted by considerations of color, sex, or nationality, it is a certainty that, overall, the average performance of those in that group will be weaker—not because of their ethnicity, of course, but because many among them were selected on grounds having no bearing on the work or study to be pursued. Preference thus creates a link between the minority preferred and inferior performance.

149

This burden is borne not only by those individuals preferred, but by every member of the minority group, including all those who genuinely excel. The general knowledge that persons with black or brown skins are given preference insures lower expectations from all whose skins are like that. Every minority member is painted with the same brush. No one—not even the minorities themselves—can know for sure that any member of a preferred group has not been given special favor; skin color, the most prominent of personal characteristics, thus becomes an inescapable onus. If some demon had sought to concoct a scheme aimed at undermining the credentials of minority businessmen, professionals, and students, to stigmatize them permanently and to humiliate them publicly, there could have been no more ingenious plan devised than the preferences now so widely given in the name of affirmative action.

Underrepresentation?

A last-ditch argument made by those favoring discrimination is that, whether or not the preferences can be justified, we must use them because otherwise certain groups will be dramatically "underrepresented" at our colleges and universities. But this is precisely the rationale that even Justice Powell rejected in another part of his *Bakke* opinion, where he wrote that ensuring a particular racial mix is nothing more than "discrimination for its own sake."

Besides, the claim is exaggerated. The students who otherwise got into top-tier schools can still go to second-tier schools—where, incidentally, they will be surrounded by students whose qualifications they more closely match. Not a bad thing: indeed, a good thing.

Roger Clegg, *National Forum: The Phi Kappa Phi Journal*, Winter 1999.

2. Unfair burdens are imposed upon individuals—deserving applicants and employees—who do not win the places they would otherwise have won because of their pale skin. One often hears the claim that the burdens of preference can be readily borne because they are so widely shared by very many among the great white majority. That is false. Most among the white majority suffer no direct loss. Those who do suffer directly are a small subset, but a subset whose members are rarely identifiable by name. If a university gives admission preference to blacks, some whites who would have been admitted but for that racial favoritism will not be admitted. We cannot learn who those persons are, but the unfairness to unidentifiable individuals who lose because of their race is nevertheless very great. Moreover, every applicant with a pale skin not admitted or appointed may rightly wonder whether it were he from whom the penalty had been exacted.

Hypocrisy and Hostility

3. Institutions that give preference pay a heavy price. Inferior performance (a consequence not of skin color but of stupid selection criteria) results in the many inefficiencies and the many hidden costs. In academic institutions, intellectual standards are lowered, explicitly or in secret; student performance is unavoidably lower, on average, than it would have been without the preferences, as is faculty productivity and satisfaction. The political need to profess equal treatment for all, while knowingly treating applicants and faculty members unequally because of their race, produces pervasive hypocrisy. Even great public institutions hide their policies, describe them deceptively, and sometimes even lie about them. This loss of integrity and public respect has been a fearful cost of race preference, from which recovery will require a generation.

4. Society at large suffers grievously from the distrust and hostility that race preference engenders. Members of ethnic groups tussling for a larger slice of the preferential pie come to distrust and despise their opposite numbers in competing minorities who (as will always appear to be the case) seem to get more than their "share" of the spoils. And fights develop over who is a member of what group, and who is entitled to its benefits. Indian tribes coming into great petroleum wealth have to develop rules for deciding what makes one a member of the tribe; is it one drop of blood? In the end we will need new Nuremberg laws and official boards to apply the rules of race membership. Ugly business.

In schools, playgrounds, and parks, in commerce and sports, in industrial employment, even in legislatures and courts, the outcome of preference is increasing racial tension and increasing self-segregation. More and more we come even to abandon the ideal of an America in which persons and not groups are the focus of praise and blame, of penalty and reward. I have been teaching at the University of Michigan since 1955; I report to you what all the talk about diversity and multiculturalism cannot hide: Preferential affirmative action on our campus (as on many campuses around the nation) has driven race relations among us to a point lower than it has ever been. The story is long and complicated and has many variants, but the short of it is this: Give preference by race and you create hostility by race. And for that we Americans are paying, and we will pay, a dreadful price.

Preference ostensibly given to overcome the legacy of racism takes the form of racism, engenders racism, nurtures racism, embitters the national community, and infects every facet of public life with racial criteria whose counterproductivity is matched only by their immorality.

> *"The overwhelming majority of American workers and managers strongly supports the affirmative action programs at their workplace."*

Affirmative Action: What Everybody Hates in Theory but Likes in Practice

Brookings Review

While surveys have concluded that a large majority of white Americans oppose affirmative action, a deeper examination of this research reveals the opposite, reports the *Brookings Review* in the following viewpoint. Many whites claim, for example, that affirmative action hurts other whites; however, they also maintain that they themselves have not been harmed by it. When asked to think about the specific affirmative action programs at their own workplaces, most Americans actually support such programs. However, the authors conclude, Americans often misrepresent their opinions on affirmative action because the media have led them to presume that it is a controversial and divisive issue.

As you read, consider the following questions:

1. According to a National Opinion Research Center poll, what percentage of Euro-Americans claim to have been personally affected by affirmative action?
2. What percentage of surveyed Americans support affirmative action programs in their own workplaces, according to a 1995 Harris poll?

Reprinted from "Affirmative Action: What Everybody Hates in Theory but Likes in Practice," *Brookings Review*, Spring 1998. Reprinted with permission from *Brookings Review*.

M ost readers and viewers of the nation's news media know from poll reports that the overwhelming majority of Americans regard affirmative action as unfair. At the same time, overwhelming support can be shown to exist for the affirmative action programs that people have experienced in person. How is this possible? The explanation lies in the profound difference between Americans' responses to survey questions about preferences in the abstract and their response to the programs they know.

In 1990 respondents to surveys by the National Opinion Research Center (NORC) of the University of Chicago were asked "What do you think the chances are these days that a white person won't get a job or promotion while an equally or less qualified Afro-American person gets one instead. Is this very likely, somewhat likely, or not very likely to happen these days?" The question was followed with probes into the reasons why the respondents held the views they did: was it "something that happened to you personally," "something that happened to a relative, family member, or close friend," something the respondent "saw occurring at work," or "heard about in the media," and so on.

In response to the speculative question, more than 70 percent of Euro-Americans asserted that other Euro-Americans were being hurt by affirmative action. But when the same group was asked not to speculate about other Euro-Americans, but to reflect on their own experience with the program, only 7 percent claimed to have been influenced by affirmative action. Fewer than one in four had heard about or witnessed anything negative concerning affirmative action at their workplace.

When a NORC poll four years later asked respondents what they themselves thought about preferences in general, again the overwhelming majority of Euro-Americans were opposed. Indeed, half of all Afro-American men opposed hypothetical preferences—a reaction that, alone, should raise questions about just what respondents imagined they were responding to.

The contrast is remarkable. When Americans speculate in the abstract about the ethics of preferential scenarios, they oppose affirmative action. When they think about the real, concrete affirmative action programs they know about and experience at their workplace, they support it. A Harris Poll in June 1995 confirmed that support. Eighty percent of Americans polled thought that their employers were doing just about the right amount, or not enough, for women and minorities.

Views on Affirmative Action

Critics of affirmative action like to cite public-opinion polls suggesting that the great majority of Americans are opposed to [it], arguing in turn that it has been extremely divisive. Defenders respond that a great deal depends on how these polls are worded: most Americans, including women and African-Americans, are opposed not to affirmative action but to quotas and to unqualified racial or gender preferences.

There is a simple way around this question. Instead of asking Americans to speculate in the abstract, one can simply ask their views about the affirmative-action programs at their own workplaces. The responses are remarkable. Over 80 percent of Euro-American workers strongly support the programs they actually know about and that directly affect them. This still does not address the issue of whether the program is in fact fair, but it does suggest that it is not undemocratic, and that a political defense of a revised version of it is possible.

Orlando Patterson, *Commentary*, March 1998.

When Americans are asked what they think about affirmative action in the abstract, they merely relay what they have read or heard in the media. The 1994 NORC poll specifically asked respondents where they had received their negative views about the program and found that the single most important source of information was the media, mentioned by 42 percent of Euro-Americans. The result has been a self-confirming media distortion of Americans' views on the subject. The media, having declared the subject controversial and divisive, then conduct polls asking respondents if the program is controversial and divisive. Respondents tell the media pollsters what they want to hear, based on what they had recently heard or read in the media. The media then report these results as further proof that the program is highly divisive.

Even more disturbing has been the media's failure to report that the overwhelming majority of American workers and managers strongly supports the affirmative action programs at their workplace. The media are by no means a disinterested player in this matter. Affirmative action programs at the nation's media organizations have been greatly resented by many established journalists—the very people who make critical decisions about what to highlight or neglect in news reports. The important 1995 Harris Poll, for example, received almost no notice from the media, a point brought to my attention by Harris Poll CEO Humphry Taylor in a personal communication. "This Harris survey," he wrote, "shows that the media have greatly overplayed the myth of the Euro-American male backlash and failed to report that the overwhelming majority of workers feel they have been treated fairly in the workplace. This is yet another case of a small, vocal minority being perceived as a majority."

Political opponents of affirmative action, being fully aware of the discrepancy between opposition to preferences posed in the abstract and support of actual affirmative action programs, exploit that discrepancy by carefully avoiding any wording that mentions affirmative action in their own campaigns against the program. Indeed, in the campaign to repeal affirmative action in California, the petition against the program went to great and successful lengths to avoid any reference to the term "affirmative action" in the wording that finally appeared on the ballot. There is now reason to believe that a significant minority of those who voted for the petition did so thinking that they were voting on behalf of affirmative action and that this group was large enough to have defeated the petition had they voted for what they thought they were voting for. California's Proposition 209 may well have been a subversion of the democratic process.

> "*Let us not do away with affirmative action so much as redefine it to make it inclusive rather than exclusive.*"

Most Americans Want to Revise Affirmative Action

Alan Wolfe

Most recent polls fail to reveal the complexity of American opinion on racism and affirmative action, argues Alan Wolfe in the following viewpoint. He maintains that while most Americans actually do oppose current affirmative action programs, a majority also agrees that racial discrimination still exists and should be addressed. What Americans really want is to revise affirmative action so that it uses fair and impartial strategies to counteract discrimination. Wolfe is the director of the Boisi Center for Religion and American Public Life at Boston College.

As you read, consider the following questions:
1. In Wolfe's opinion, how do middle-class Americans differ from intellectuals in discussions about affirmative action?
2. According to the author, what criterion do both critics and supporters of affirmative action agree on?
3. In the author's view, why are most ordinary Americans unconcerned about the fact that affirmative action was never subject to a popular vote?

Reprinted from "Is Affirmative Action on the Way Out? Should It Be?" by Alan Wolfe, *Commentary*, March 1998. Reprinted with permission from *Commentary* and the author. All rights reserved.

One way of thinking about affirmative action . . . runs as follows. Classifying by race has always been a policy without a popular mandate. Contrary to the color-blind language of the Civil Rights Act of 1964, lawyers and bureaucrats instituted affirmative action by way of regulation. It follows that the public debate we are having on the subject will result in the abolition of the policy, for Americans never have, and do not now, support the philosophy behind it.

Those who think this way had better not bet the ranch on public opinion. It is true that polls show overwhelming opposition to quotas and preferences. But polling may not be the best way to measure how people really make up their minds on any complex and contentious issue. In an effort to shed light on the way Americans consider their moral obligations, I recently completed 200 in-depth interviews with middle-class suburbanites around Tulsa, Boston, San Diego, and Atlanta. (The interviews form the basis of my book, *One Nation, After All*.) One of the issues I discussed with them was affirmative action.

A More Nuanced Picture

My study, at first glance, shows that the polls are correct: in a vain effort to avoid using loaded terms, I asked people whether, in their view, African-Americans should have "priority" in jobs or college admissions because of past discrimination. Irrespective of race, nearly all my respondents said no. But as I allowed people to express the moral reasoning that went into their responses, a more nuanced picture emerged.

Few of the middle-class Americans with whom I spoke were in doubt that racism in America is quite real. One of them, a Christian conservative living in Broken Arrow, Oklahoma, learned his lessons about racial discrimination not from liberals but from black preachers working for the Promise Keepers, an evangelical movement dedicated to ensuring that men keep their promises to their wives and children. Another conservative Christian, this time from Cobb County, Georgia, said he was an enthusiastic supporter of Newt Gingrich, but also added that anyone would have to be a "fool" to think that racism did not exist.

Interviews like these suggest a lesson concerning how we

talk about affirmative action. When intellectuals debate the issue, they tend to divide themselves into Left and Right, with the former insisting on the persistence of racism and the latter suggesting significant racial progress. In the heartland, I believe, people transcend such categories when they think about race. They rely on experience, not political ideology, to guide their views. And most people know from experience that discrimination still exists.

The Importance of Merit

The question of experience is also central to a second way in which the middle-class Americans with whom I spoke differ from intellectuals. The debate among intellectuals over affirmative action is really a debate about merit. Those for whom merit remains the primary criterion for distributing jobs and places in schools are the most vehement opponents of affirmative action. Defenders of those policies often respond by suggesting that social values other than merit—for example, diverse workplace and educational environments—sometimes have to trump meritocratic principles.

Among the people with whom I spoke, by contrast, merit was the fundamental moral criterion relied on by both critics and supporters of affirmative action. Needless to say, opponents of affirmative action did not like the fact that students who score lower on tests or who have less job experience are admitted to college or promoted at the expense of the more gifted. Such practices so clearly violate standards of fairness based on merit that they needed no further amplification. Unexpected was the merit-based reasoning of some of those who defended affirmative action. "My skin color automatically subtracts 10 percent from my merits," said a black minister in DeKalb County, Georgia, who went on to defend affirmative action on the grounds that it restores the 10 percent and in that way allows him to compete on an equal playing field with whites. Another black suburbanite in Georgia spoke this way: "I'm not saying that we need affirmative action to erase 400 years of slavery and all that," but because white employers occasionally pass over more qualified blacks to hire whites out of prejudice, "sometimes there are people who need to be forced to make the right decision." Although disagreements were real, they were not over irreconcilable principles but instead over the empirical question of how to ensure that the best people get the right jobs.

Philosophical Versus Practical Arguments

A final way in which the debate over affirmative action among intellectuals differs from the debate taking place in middle-class America concerns the legitimacy of law. For critics of the policy, the very fact that affirmative action was never subject to a popular vote raises questions about its legitimacy. In a 1979 article critical of affirmative action, Carl Cohen argued that attempts to clothe the compulsory nature of the policy by calling it voluntary avoided "the key question of legitimate authority." For Cohen, citizens have fundamental rights, including the right to equal treatment regardless of race, and if government takes those rights away, as, in his view, it was doing under most affirmative-action programs, government must either lie about what it is doing or, if it is honest about its intentions, admit that it has exceeded what it may legitimately do.

Mending Affirmative Action

As the sociologist Jerome Karabel reminds us, while it is true that Americans worry about "quotas" and about "unqualified" people being hired, promoted, and admitted to colleges and universities, they also recognize "that the playing field is not level and that programs are needed to ensure equal opportunities for minorities and women." That probably explains why, following President Bill Clinton's 1995 speech on affirmative action, two national opinion polls, despite slightly different wording, found that 60 to 65 percent of American voters approved of the President's position that affirmative action should be mended and not ended.

William Julius Wilson, *American Prospect*, September/October 1999.

No one with whom I spoke, no matter how strongly he may have opposed affirmative action, resorted to a language of legitimacy. Opponents of affirmative action tended to be those most respectful of law. The fact that affirmative action was not the result of true democratic decision-making was not salient to them because, in their cynicism about politics, they did not think that very many policies were ever subject to proper democratic decision-making. The opponents of affirmative action with whom I spoke wanted to see the policy changed, but, once again, more for practical than for philosophical reasons.

Nor did all of them want to see it changed. One respondent, a policeman in Oklahoma, said matter-of-factly: "I can understand, like, going into minority neighborhoods, it's better to have a minority officer." And what about women, I asked him? "Yeah, I've seen people, they tend to obey a woman officer better." This man, who had no political ideology, simply wanted to know what the law was, so that the best job of enforcing it could be done.

Perhaps the last word on the subject should be given to a post-office manager in Eastlake, California. "I think affirmative action is good," he said, "but I think it should be for everybody." A bit stunned, my research assistant asked him whether he meant that affirmative action should be based on class, not race. "No," he replied. "I think affirmative action should be based on the whole populace. In other words, not just one segment of the population. Not, for example, just women alone for affirmative action. I think it should be for everyone, for all races, all genders, all citizens." It is not clear that this man understood what affirmative action is. But in his own way, he understood something about America: let us not do away with affirmative action so much as redefine it to make it inclusive rather than exclusive.

Seeking a "Soft Landing"

After listening to so many Americans, I am convinced that most of them do not like affirmative action and think its time has come to an end. But I am also persuaded that they want to find a "soft landing," one that would take cognizance of rightful claims by African-Americans about merit and discrimination. It is not clear what policy implications follow from their views, although my understanding is that their sense of fairness would not be violated by any program that tried informally to expand those networks that are important to jobs, promotions, and college admissions for those, especially African-Americans, who lack access to them.

I do not report these findings to argue that intellectuals are debating affirmative action wrongly; it is the task of philosophers, lawyers, and polemicists to argue for what they believe to be right. But I do think a warning is in order. Conservatives . . . took the lead in contending that, in their enthusiasm for welfare, or their disdain for the victims of crime, liberal intellectuals had become so out of touch with public opinion that they constituted a "new class," unwilling to test their ideas in the hard realities of democratic politics. It would be truly ironic if opponents of affirmative action—convinced that such programs are immoral and insistent that they be abolished "cold turkey"—were to ignore the sentiments of people in the country who may agree with them in theory but who also, in practice, want to keep at least some version of affirmative action that would guarantee fairness and overcome whatever racial discrimination remains.

Periodical Bibliography

The following articles have been selected to supplement the diverse views presented in this chapter. Addresses are provided for periodicals not indexed in the *Readers' Guide to Periodical Literature*, the *Alternative Press Index*, the *Social Sciences Index*, or the *Index to Legal Periodicals and Books*.

William C. Bowen and Derek Bok
"The Proof Is in the Pudding," *Washington Post National Weekly Edition*, September 28, 1998. Available from 1150 15th St. NW, Washington, DC 20071.

Paul Butler, interviewed by Lloyd Eby
"Race *Should* Be Used for Governmental Decision-Making," *World & I*, September 1998. Available from 3600 New York Ave. NE, Washington, DC 20002.

Roger Clegg
"Beyond Quotas," *Policy Review*, May/June 1998.

Ruth Bader Ginsberg
"Affirmative Action as an International Human Rights Dialogue," *Brookings Review*, Winter 2000.

Nathan Glazer
"In Defense of Preference," *New Republic*, August 6, 1998.

Glenn C. Loury
"Color-Blinded," *New Republic*, August 17-24, 1998.

D.W. Miller
"Opportunity Without Preference," *Policy Review*, November/December 1998.

Orlando Patterson
"Affirmative Action: Opening Up Workplace Networks to Afro-Americans," *Brookings Review*, Spring 1998.

David Shipler
"Reflections on Race," *Tikkun*, January/February 1998.

Thomas Sowell
"Misshapen Statistics on Racial Quotas," *American Spectator*, April 1999.

Shelby Steele
"How Liberals Debase Black Achievement," *Policy Review*, November/December 1998.

Stephan Thernstrom and Abigail Thernstrom
"Racial Preferences: What We Now Know," *Commentary*, February 1999.

CHAPTER 4

How Should Society View Interracial Families?

Chapter Preface

Interracial families in the United States have been on the increase through marriage, birth, and adoption. Between 1960 and 1992, for example, the number of interracial marriages multiplied more than seven times over. Although black-white unions are still fairly uncommon, accounting for about 20 percent of all interracial marriages, other kinds of multiethnic pairings have become the norm. More than half of the U.S. marriages involving people of Japanese descent, for instance, are intermarriages with whites.

Many people feel positive about the increase in interracial marriages, maintaining that multiethnic families transcend race by unifying people through love, respect, and common humanity. These optimists believe that interracial families will dismantle racism as they bring different cultures together in kinship. As syndicated commentator Scott London states, "The mingling and the mixing of race is a sign that we are evolving to a higher, more integrated state as a culture. . . . I look upon the hybridization of America as a source of great promise. The future belongs to the mestizo, the person who straddles many different worlds and can help explain them to each other."

Others are not so sure that mixed-race families herald the end of distinctions based on color or ethnic ancestry. *Newsweek* columnist Ellis Cose maintains that racism persists in multiethnic societies: "Even in Brazil, where racial mixing is . . . celebrated, color coding has not lost its sting. Status and privilege are still connected to lighter skin. Racial distinctions . . . are constantly made. In the emerging U.S. mestizo future, some people will still be whiter than others—and if the Latin American experience is any guide, they will have an advantage."

In the United States today, interracial families may not represent the elimination of racial differences, prejudices, and stereotypes. Nevertheless, as the following chapter shows, these families are challenging racial divisions in profound ways.

"*Intermarriage encourages the learning of transracial empathy that is crucial for enabling people to place themselves in the shoes of others racially different than themselves.*"

Interracial Marriages Should Be Encouraged

Randall Kennedy

In the following viewpoint, Harvard University law professor Randall Kennedy asserts that interracial marriages, particularly marriages between blacks and whites, should be promoted. Such intermarriage will help to dismantle racism as a growing number of blacks and whites build kinships across society's traditional racial boundaries, writes Kennedy. Interracial couples do still face hostile opposition from both whites and nonwhites, he explains, but their efforts to develop loving transracial bonds are to be encouraged and applauded.

As you read, consider the following questions:
1. According to Kennedy, what statute did Richard and Mildred Loving violate?
2. In 1990, what percentage of married blacks had a white spouse?
3. What three steps should be taken to encourage interracial marriage, in the author's opinion?

Excerpted from "How Are We Doing With Loving," by Randall Kennedy, *Interrace*, vol. 9, no. 3, 1999. Reprinted with permission from the author.

The historical U.S. Supreme Court case titled *Loving v. Virginia* arose from the fact that in 1958, two Virginians, Richard Loving and Mildred Jeter, married one another in Washington, D.C. and then returned to their native state to live together as man and wife. The problem was that Richard was white and Mildred was black and that the state of Virginia outlawed such marriages.

The "Racial Purity" Law

Virginia had barred interracial marriages continuously since 1691 when it restricted English persons from intermarrying with Negroes, mulattos, or Indians to prevent the "abominable mixture and spurious issue" that were fearfully expected from such unions. The statute under which the Lovings were prosecuted was enacted in 1924. Entitled "An Act to Preserve Racial Purity," the law narrowed existing racial definitions of whiteness and decreed that in Virginia no white person could marry anyone other than another white person. Not only did this law criminalize interracial marriage within the state; it also criminalized entering into an interracial marriage outside the state with the intent of evading Virginia's prohibition.

The Act to Preserve Racial Purity also declared that an interracial marriage was void which meant, among other things, that children born to such a union were deemed in the eyes of the state to be illegitimate and without the protections and privileges accorded to the children of lawfully wedded parents.

The Lovings pleaded guilty to violating the Act to Preserve Racial Purity and were sentenced to one year in jail, though the trial judge gave them the option of avoiding incarceration on the condition that they leave the state and not return together for 25 years. In the course of the proceedings the trial judge asserted that "Almighty God created the races white, black, yellow, malay and red, and he placed them on separate continents. And but for the interference with his arrangement there would be no cause for such marriages. The fact that he separated the races shows that he did not intend for the races to mix."

After Virginia's Supreme Court of Appeals affirmed the

conviction, the Supreme Court of the United States reversed it on the grounds that the federal constitution prohibits states from barring interracial marriage. In the process of doing so, the Court also implicitly invalidated similar laws then in existence in 15 other states.

The Supreme Court issued its ruling on June 12, 1967. Given that more than 30 years has elapsed since that landmark decision, it seems appropriate to ask how we are doing with *Loving*.

After the *Loving* Ruling

Loving occupies a totally secure niche in American constitutional law. Its significance is sufficiently vibrant to have caused a principal to lose his job in Wedowee, Alabama for voicing opposition to interracial dating and marriage, and that such relationships have become sufficiently acceptable that by 1991 Senator Strom Thurmond, once a fire-eating segregationist, debated unreservedly on behalf of the imperiled Supreme Court nomination of Clarence Thomas, a black man who resided in Virginia and lived in married bliss with a white woman.

In the post-*Loving* regime, at least in terms of race, no one has to worry about governments counteracting or prohibiting desires to marry.

So how are we doing with *Loving?* Although the marriage market remains racially segmented, white-black marriages have increased. According to the calculations of Douglas Besharov and Timothy Sullivan, in 1960, about 1.7% of married blacks had a white spouse. In 1990, the percentage had risen to about 5.9%. Moreover, the pace of increase in marriage across the black-white racial frontier is quickening, especially in terms of white men and black women. (In 1980, black women married white men in only 0.7% of all marriages involving a black bride; by 1993, black women were marrying white men in 3.9% of the marriages involving black brides.) . . .

The pattern of intermarriage of other peoples of color with whites has increased over time. Of marriages involving a person of Japanese ancestry in the 1940s, for example, about 10 to 15 percent involved intermarriages with whites.

By the 1960s, nearly half of the marriages involving a person of Japanese ancestry involved intermarriages with whites. There has been a lesser degree of intermarriage with other groups, such as people of Chinese and Korean ancestry. But the rates at which individuals in these groups intermarry with whites has always been greater than white-black rates of intermarriage. There is considerable reluctance to view the relatively low rates of black-white intermarriage as a problem.

Concerns About White-Black Intermarriage

One source of reluctance is a desire to avoid nourishing an already swollen racial self-importance that afflicts many whites; some people understandably fear that suggesting intimate association with whites as a valuable commodity will only heighten the vice of white racial pride.

Another source of reluctance is that portraying low rates of white-black intermarriage as a problem will reinforce longstanding beliefs that blacks lack a decent sense of racial self-respect and want nothing more than to become intimate, especially sexually intimate, with whites.

The Path to a Better World

Far from being a sign of deviance, intermarriage is an indication of enlightenment and the path to a better world. From their perspective those who intermarry are at the forefront of the breakdown of intergroup barriers, models for a future world where people will no longer divide themselves by antiquated and dangerous cultural identities. Through their choice the cross-cultural couple validates the universality of the human condition. Their relationships will lead to a creative and life-enhancing genetic, cultural, and spiritual cross-fertilization.

J. Crohn, *Mixed Matches: How to Create Successful Interracial, Interethnic, and Interfaith Marriages*, 1995.

A third source of reluctance stems from the sense that marriage should be based upon tender feelings of love therefore it occupies a wholly different plane than jobs, or housing, or schooling or any of the other institutions, goods, or services that are the typical subjects of debate in discussions over race relations policy.

Each of these concerns point towards political and analytical difficulties that make the subject of white-black intermarriage treacherous terrain. In my view, however, the relative fewness of white-black intermarriages is an important problem that warrants attention and discussion. That blacks intermarry with whites at strikingly lower rates than others is yet another sign of the uniquely encumbered and peculiarly isolated status of African Americans.

It is also an obstacle to the development of attitudes and connections that will be necessary to improve the position of black Americans and, beyond that, to address the racial divisions that continue to hobble our nation. Marriage matters. That is why white supremacists invested so much time, thought, and energy into prohibiting marriage across racial lines. Marriage plays a large role in governing the intergenerational transfer of wealth. It also is central to maintaining a stable race line. After all, when people intermarry and produce children of mixed race, racial identifications, racial loyalties, and racial kinships blur.

Why Interracial Marriage Is Good

Granted the social significance of intermarriage, what should one's stance toward it be? In my view, white-black intermarriage is not simply something that should be tolerated. It is a type of partnership that should be applauded and encouraged.

Intermarriage is good because it signals that newcomers or outsiders are gaining acceptance in the eyes of those in the dominant population and are perceived by them as persons of value. Intermarriage is also good because it breaks down the psychological boundaries that distance people on racial grounds, opening up new expectations and experiences that would otherwise remain hidden.

Intermarriage encourages the learning of transracial empathy that is crucial for enabling people to place themselves in the shoes of others racially different than themselves. Few situations are more likely to mobilize the racially-privileged individual to move against racial wrongs than witnessing such wrongs inflicted upon his mother-in-law, father-in-law, spouse, or child. Fortified by such lessons and animated by a newly drawn map of racial self-interest, participants in interracial marriage are likely to fight against racial wrongs that menace loved ones.

Opposition to Intermarriage

There are, of course, powerful forces against increased rates of white-black intermarriage. One impediment is the residual influence of white opposition. Some polls suggest that as much as 20% of the white population continues to believe that interracial marriage should be illegal. Some of these people express their disapproval in ways that go beyond answering the questions of pollsters. Through stares, catcalls, and even violence, they put a shadow over interracial intimacy, driving up its costs and frightening off some who might otherwise explore its possibilities.

It is a terrible fact that in many locales, mixed couples face a substantial risk that they will be subjected to abuse by those who feel affronted by a form of loving that they perceive as "unnatural."

A second impediment is the centrifugal force of black solidarity. In *Mixed Blood*, an illuminating study of intermarriage that focuses on Jews, blacks, and Japanese Americans, Paul R. Spickard writes:

> [W]here there were clusters of Black people, Japanese Americans, or Jews along with ethnic institutions such as synagogues and fraternal organizations, the communities actively discouraged intermarriage. . . . Where such social networks were lacking, individuals were more likely to override any personal internal constraints and marry outside the group.

Blacks who intermarry with whites can expect to be viewed with skepticism, if not hostility, by many other blacks who will consider them to be racial defectors. It does not matter that there are many examples of blacks who, though intermarried with whites, have consistently and militantly fought to improve the fortunes of African Americans; Frederick Douglass, Walter White, Richard Wright, James Farmer, and Marian Wright Edelman, for example.

A third impediment has to do with the brutal consequences of deprivation: the fact that, because of historical and ongoing oppression, many blacks will simply have less to offer in the marriage market. Black people live shorter lives, typically have less education, are objects of discrimination, and face all manners of racial obstacles in the struggle for upward mobility. The extent to which this is true, blacks will seem less of a "good catch" to many people, particularly whites, in the marriage market. Marriage often involves an entire array of delicate and mysterious feelings and motivations—lust, love, and the deepest springs of self-identity—however, marriage also triggers concerns about dollars and cents, social advancement, finding a good catch.

As long as black people are kept in a state of relative social, political, and economic deprivation, others will be less inclined to want to marry them. What is to be done?

Encouraging Interracial Relationships

First, the legal system ought to carry through completely with the anti-discrimination agenda. . . .

Second, people who embrace my view should openly and unapologetically express their opinion on the subject to their mothers and fathers, sisters and brothers, colleagues and friends. Consider the following scenario: A white man friend lets it be known that he would like to be introduced to a nice woman. It just so happens that around the same time a black woman friend indicates that she would like to be introduced to a nice man.

My impression is that many people would steer the white man to a white woman and the black woman to a black man. What one should do is introduce these two people to one another as potential romantic partners. Furthermore, if, after the blind date, either party complains about the racial politics of the matchmaking, people of my ideological persuasion should openly, calmly, but resolutely question the basis of the complaint and through discussion attempt to persuade friends to reconsider whether they want to remain committed to inherited conventions and formulas that limit their choice of potential partners.

Finally, people should militantly support policies that elevate the status of black Americans. The more secure, accepted, and prosperous they are, the more attractive they will be in the marriage market, further spurring the modest increase in intermarriage that we have witnessed over the past decade. This will help to bring about the type of society I want: a cosmopolitan society in which race no longer impedes the ability of people to appreciate the human qualities of one another, a society in which interracial loving is not only tolerated but so normal that it ceases to be an object of sensational wonderment.

The coming of this society will be both heralded and made possible by more interracial marriages. That is why I support the practice—not simply tolerate it but encourage it. That is also why I look back on *Loving v. Virginia* with gratitude, and hope that more people will take advantage of this enlarged area of freedom.

| *"Let's not forget that when it comes to bridging the gap of race, love isn't all we need."*

Interracial Marriages Will Not Eliminate Racism

Eric Liu

Many have argued that interracial marriage will heal racial strife in America, writes Eric Liu in the following viewpoint. He maintains, however, that while intermarriage may exemplify a love that transcends racial barriers, it does not have a significant impact on racism. Despite increasing numbers of interracial families, Liu points out, racial stereotypes—such as the belief that lighter skin color is more desirable—are still prevalent. He concludes that racism is more effectively battled in the domain of public politics than in the domain of romance. Liu is a freelance journalist and the author of *The Accidental Asian: Notes of a Native Speaker*.

As you read, consider the following questions:

1. How many mixed-race unions currently exist, according to Liu?
2. According to the author, which notable historical figures have promoted miscegenation?
3. What kind of interracial marriage is the least common, states Liu?

Reprinted from "Mingling Bloodlines Isn't Enough to Bridge the Race Gap," by Eric Liu, *USA Today*, July 11, 1998. Reprinted with permission from the author.

Sometimes, as my wife and I walk down the street, we'll notice a couple coming the other way. We won't do anything to indicate that we've seen them. We won't make eye contact. But immediately after they pass, Carroll and I will give each other a nudge.

"BRC," we'll whisper. As in "biracial couple."

Now, this may sound a little odd. Or unduly color-conscious. Or maybe even prejudiced. But you see, it isn't with disapproval that we notice BRCs. After all, we are one. Carroll is Scotch-Irish and Jewish; I am Chinese. And we are conscious of other mixed couples; we practically tally them up because there's something undeniably satisfying about encountering fellow trespassers of the color line.

For one thing, there's a sense of solidarity, the feeling that this other couple might know, on some level, how we relate to the world. There's also, I have to say, a sense of confidence, perhaps even smugness—a feeling that we are the wave of the future, ahead of the demographic curve.

An Increase in Mixed-Race Unions

There was a time, of course, when racial intermarriage was strictly prohibited, whether by law or by custom. And to be sure, most marriages today are still unmixed. But Americans are intermarrying more today than ever before. The number of mixed-race unions has increased from 150,000 in 1960 to over 1.5 million today; the number of multiracial kids has boomed to more than 2 million.

And so it's not surprising that one of the central points of Warren Beatty's farcical film *Bulworth* is that mixing up our genes (Sen. Bulworth puts it more colorfully) is the way to move the country beyond color. As Beatty said in a recent interview, there's a simple solution to the race problem: "It's called love."

This "love" line is an old riff. Throughout our history, people from Alexis De Tocqueville to Frederick Douglass to Norman Podhoretz have proclaimed that miscegenation is the only true path to interracial healing.

It's certainly a nice thought. As one who has jumped into the integrated gene pool, I'd like to think I'm doing my part to advance good race relations. But it's misguided, in the end, to say that the difference I make is the difference that matters.

We can start by asking a simple question: What is the problem that intermarriage is supposed to solve? If the problem is strife between races, well sure, BRCs are powerful symbols of life beyond pure hostility. But generally, BRCs aren't trying to save the world; they just happened to fall in love. And their mere existence doesn't do much to alter the social circumstances—from residential segregation to media stereotypes to campaign rhetoric—that can generate racial hostility.

If the problem is something else—say, that people of color are vulnerable to discrimination—it's not clear that BRCs solve the problem at all. It's true, of course, that mixed marriages produce mixed kids and that mixed children defy old racial categories. It's not necessarily true, though, that the collapse of racial categories means the collapse of racialism.

Not a Political Statement

Dating Patrick was neither a political, artistic, or rebellious choice.

Yes, I am grateful for political statements that encourage tolerance; they have their place.

And yes, I do notice the aesthetic beauty of our contrasting color; his dark skin with my light coloring.

And it is true that I sometimes want to rebel against old traditions and systems that no longer seem helpful, but choosing to be with Patrick was nothing that complex. It was perhaps the most primitive of human decisions.

It was falling in love; finding a life partner, that warm secure feeling of waking up one morning and not wanting to date anyone else but him.

Valerie Rhodes, *Interrace*, Winter 1998.

Consider how "blacks," who are as genetically mixed a group as can be found in America, were converted by a "one-drop rule" into a single group. Think about how those Asian-Americans who are assimilating and intermarrying are said now to be "becoming white."

And note that while intermarriage is up across the board, mixed marriages involving blacks are still the least common.

Perhaps our color line is giving way to a color continuum. But life along that continuum is still likely to follow a simple rule: The lighter you are, the better. When Carroll and I have kids, will they be considered white? Will they be called Asian? Will they be more stigmatized than "pure" whites and Asians? Will they be less stigmatized than other mixed children with darker skin?

Intermarriage Is No Panacea

The answers lie not in what is to be seen but in how people choose to see. Intermarriage isn't the panacea we'd like it to be, but it does make one thing clear: Race is a man-made myth, not a God-given truth, and it's something we impose upon each other often in spite of our actual color.

That's why it falls to that other timeless pursuit—politics, rather than procreation—to address the fact that in countless unwanted ways, race still matters. It's in the realm of public life, not the realm of personal romance, that we can do most to equalize the life chances of kids of every hue.

So by all means, let's mingle our blood lines with abandon. Let's hurry forth the day when counting BRCs is a tired game. But let's not forget that when it comes to bridging the gap of race, love isn't all we need.

*"Growing up as biracial . . . acquainted me
. . . with racial prejudice rooted in all
aspects of Latino and American culture."*

Biracial Children Often Have Difficult Lives

Marta I. Cruz-Janzen

In the following viewpoint, Marta I. Cruz-Janzen maintains that biracial children face considerable difficulties because society is obsessed with rigid racial boundaries. These boundaries exacerbate tensions within and between different racial groups, she points out, creating complex dilemmas for multiracial individuals. Though biracial children are part of two cultures, they are often ostracized and rejected by both. If biracial children do gain acceptance, it is usually as a result of rejecting half of their background, writes Cruz-Janzen. She concludes that society must shed its rigid racial distinctions if these children are to have any hope of claiming their full identity. Cruz-Janzen is an assistant professor in the department of secondary education at the Metropolitan State College of Denver. She is also coauthor of *Educating Young Children in a Diverse Society*.

As you read, consider the following questions:
1. What is the historical objective of American citizenship, in the author's opinion?
2. According to Cruz-Janzen, why do many black immigrants deny any connection to African Americans?
3. In what way does the desire for Caucasian physical features create tension within racial and ethnic groups, according to the author?

Reprinted from "It's Not Just Black and White: Who Are the Other 'Others'?" by Marta I. Cruz-Janzen, *Interrace*, Fall 1998.

We live with a "box mentality." We sort and box people into racial categories set by rigid boundaries between groups. These boundaries exacerbate the tension within groups and between them. I am Latinegra. Both my parents are Puerto Rican; one black, the other, white. The U.S. has lumped all Latinos, from Latin America, North America, and Spain together as "Hispanics," ignoring the vast cultural, economic, language, national, political, and racial diversity that exists within this classification. Growing up as biracial, between Puerto Rico and the mainland, acquainted me, at an early age, with racial prejudice rooted in all aspects of Latino and American culture.

Accordingly, multiracial Americans are pressured to fit neatly and quietly within one of four racial boxes; many of us getting tossed from box to box.

In 1993, an Hispanic reader from New Mexico wrote to *Hispanic* magazine, in response to earlier coverage of Latino major league baseball players which included black Latinos: "I would appreciate knowing how the writer arrived at the classification of apparent blacks as Hispanics? Does the fact that these men come from Spanish-speaking countries such as Puerto Rico or Cuba automatically give them the Hispanic designation? History shows that Africans were transported to the Americas as slaves and took the names of their slave masters."

The resounding attitude among some Hispanics/Latinos is that I am not one of them because of my "one-drop" of "black blood."

Caught Between Two Worlds

"Hispanics are from Spain," an Hispanic educator told me two years ago. "You are not Hispanic. You are black." In other words, "How dare *you* speak Spanish and claim to be one of us."

Although family and friends call me *triguena* (wheat-colored), I recall the cruel taunts of classmates, adults, and even teachers. I was repeatedly called *negativo* (photo negative) because while I resemble my mother, I am black and she is white. Being called *Perlina* was supposed to be a compliment. Perlina was a popular bleaching detergent with the picture of black children dressed in white on the label: I was a bleached black person. Due to my biracial heritage, I stood out among my classmates. They teased that I was *"una mosca en un vaso de leche"* (A fly in a glass of milk).

A high school teacher in New York advised me to identify as black because "that's how others will see you and that's how you will be treated, even by Latinos." Yet, there are Puerto Ricans and other Latinos who insist that I am *not* black. In fact, some scold me for being "too black" and advise me to be more Latina instead.

African Americans don't necessarily accept me either because I "don't understand or think like black folks." Ironically, they also tell me that I am ashamed of my black heritage by claiming to be Latina and speaking Spanish. They urge me to finally accept who I am. "Puerto Ricans are nothing but black folks in hiding."

Race Is a Political Construct

My experience with others and how they perceive me is frustrating and painful; one that is common for an increasing number of multiracial Latinos, caught in the race wars that mar our country. Americans have a strong need to categorize and segregate—to sustain the white majority and oppress "weaker" minorities. While this is common to all human societies, color, race, and ethnicity in America have become uniquely political.

Our society designates multiracial individuals, although many are part white—some predominantly white—as "persons of color," at the same time making them undesirable to all parties because they do not unequivocally fit in the categorical box. Part-white multiracial Americans are pushed to identify with their communities of color where they are similarly not accepted. Multiracial persons with two "ethnic" parents, are also rejected by both groups, though they are pushed to identify with the group of lower social status.

In addition to being denied full and equal membership into various groups, multiracial persons are forced to choose between groups.

A 26-year-old multiracial woman of Anglo-American and white Latino heritage recalls the rejection by her American white friends after being labeled Hispanic in high school: "I wasn't one of them. Suddenly, I was different." She recalls the frustration: "I didn't get along with this side and I didn't get along with that side. . . . no matter what I did somebody was always mad at me." To gain the acceptance of Latinos, she had to practically renounce her Anglo-American heritage. Furthermore, "I had to tell 'whitey' jokes," even ones directed toward her father.

Mainstream American society is obsessed with whiteness and the exclusion of anyone who is not of anglo descent. It has created a caste system whereby Anglo-Americans are elevated to the highest status relative to that of "others."

The historical objective of American citizenship is assimilation—the process whereby "minority" groups shed their ethnic heritage and ultimately adopt the standards established by the Anglo-American majority.

A young woman of Anglo-American and white Latino heritage expressed her fears: "I fit in [with whites] because of the way I look . . . I had to be white. I couldn't be Latino too." She knew that she would be "ostracized somehow" if she revealed her Latino heritage. Those who cannot blend in become "something else"—something *other* than white—which includes Spaniards and their descendants.

"Africa begins in the Pyrenees" is a European expression which clearly reflects disdain for both Africa and Spain. With a long history of interracial unions before they set sail for the Americas, Spaniards and Latinos are considered racially impure; unfitting for membership in the global white world.

African ancestry (as little as "one-drop") is perceived by whites and, in fact, most non-white groups as the bottom-most on the racial pole. Newcomers to America learn this quickly and move as far away from any black likening as possible, physically and psychologically. Many black immigrants from around the world, including the darkest black Latinos, disavow any connection to African Americans.

The "American Culture" Myth

American culture has additionally promoted the myth that all Europeans share an un-ethnic "American culture." Ethnic issues become the concern of others and multicultural education, the study of "minorities." To be American and white is to be "normal." All others—the so-called minorities—are abnormal and un-American. A young woman, whose father is white Latino and whose mother is white American, stated her white fiancé's nervousness about her dual heritage and recounted a "huge argument" they had because he insisted that she was not biracial since she had blonde hair and blue eyes. "You are white," he concluded.

As an educator, and particularly an elementary school principal, I witnessed the acrimonious politics of ethnic and racial group membership and rejection played out at all school levels. For instance, a fourth grader, who was often in my office for verbal and physical aggression against both teachers and classmates, was, after several years, able to put into words his anguish. This son, of a Mexican American father and Anglo-American mother, hated his parents "for having me." In a predominantly Latino school, he was a social outcast, jeered by classmates, called a "white boy." His parents, especially his mother, were the objects of derisive jokes.

Social Outcasts

A 26-year-old multiracial woman of white Latino and Native American parentage expressed similar anger. "Why did they [parents] have me? Didn't they think that this was going to be so hard? Who were they to decide my fate?"

A multiracial adult male whose mother is white Latino and whose father is Anglo-American recalled crying inconsolably at recess when he was young. "I would go off by myself in a corner and cry. I didn't have any friends. Nobody liked me." He wanted to be like everybody else. He reminds me of a second grader of Mexican American and African American parentage who would also cry and cry in my office unable to tell me why except she had no friends and nobody liked her either.

I can still hear the anguished cry of a beautiful multiracial middle school student of black Latino and white Latino ancestry who was called "ape man" and "jungle bunny" by her peers. She left for school one morning feeling on top of the world wearing a new outfit; her hair professionally styled for the first time. She thought her classmates would compliment her. Instead, they—especially Latino boys—insisted that no matter what she did to herself, she still looked like a monkey; she was still ugly. They threw water all over her new clothes and hair.

Another Mexican-African American recalls being rejected by her community. "I was looked down upon because I thought I was Mexican. They'd make fun of my hair, the thickness of my hair. They would call me nigger, black, and other names. The boys let me know that they didn't think I was attractive. The Mexican girls were really mean—evil. They were my friends but they would not allow me to be Mexican. They would always let me know that I wasn't like them—I wasn't Mexican."

A high school teenager of black Latino and white Latino parentage walked out of school and came home crying to tell her parents that she no longer wanted to return. That day a teacher in her predominantly white school taught that [all] black people had been brought to America as slaves. Her peers taunted her. They called her nigger, slave, pushed and shoved her, and ordered her around.

In a predominantly Latino middle school, a child of African American and Latino Indian ancestry was sent to the office for fighting at recess. During geography class her peers insisted that it was O.K. for whites to call blacks niggers because black people had named themselves that. There is a country [Niger] in Africa named after them, they insisted.

Racial Hostility

Certainly not all multiracial Latinos are barraged with insults and objection. But very few escape the narrow-minded legacy of slavery and bigotry. My own child, then in middle school, pleaded that her Anglo-American father not attend a school program for fear that her black and Latino friends would see him. White students had rejected her, together with other black and Latino students. Her friends knew I was Latinegra but they did not know her father was white.

Ours is a culture that confers preferential treatment on lighter-skinned individuals, further pitting people of color against each other, within and between groups—and certainly within families. White attributes, such as long, straight hair, thin lips, and refined nose shapes, are more attractive and desirable. The coveting of whiteness also leads to resentment within and between "ethnic" groups. Indeed, lighter skin may be more desirable, but it is also equated with possessing the blood of the enemy. While trying to promote their own superiority, darker-skinned people resent their lighter-skinned members, especially those of multiracial heritage.

The mainstream school environment is often ethnically and racially hostile to students of color, but especially multiracial students who have no on-campus support system. Most of the antagonism and abuse of multiracial children occurs in the school environment. Furthermore, teachers and students alike insist that multiracial students identify exclusively with one group, primarily the group with the lowest social status. As a result, multiracial students are often harassed and rejected by all sides.

Identification Is a Human Right

Though much debate continues to take place within some communities about the pros and cons of a multiracial category . . . the fact is that this is not an exclusive "black and white" issue. Yet, the debate continues in almost complete disregard for the historical background of racism in the creation of racial and ethnic labels, and the fact that the rapidly growing multiracial population today is not solely of black and white backgrounds, but of various multicolored unions.

Persons of multiple ethnic and racial heritage no longer want to be invisible—accepted by none, condemned and rejected by all. Certainly, for the sake of our children, multiracial individuals must exist as valid members of humanity and demand inclusion, legitimacy, and recognition. Not until all Americans are granted the basic human right of self-identification in a diverse society will we shed our "box mentality" and break the shackles of psychological slavery that still bind us; the shackles that create bosses and servants, slave masters and slaves, and superior and inferior human beings. Only then will we be able to sit together at the American table as one.

> "Contrary to popular belief, being born into
> a biracial home does not automatically
> condemn one to a life of isolation and ethnic
> schizophrenia."

Biracial Children Can Have Rich Lives

Susan Fales-Hill

Growing up biracial is not the miserable experience that many have claimed, writes Susan Fales-Hill in the following viewpoint. Recalling her childhood with a white father and Haitian mother in a New York multiethnic enclave, Fales-Hill maintains that she feels enriched by her racially mixed background. Although the life of a biracial child may not be free of racial turmoil, Fales-Hill contends, many mixed-race individuals learn to embrace all aspects of their identity and become well-adjusted adults. Fales-Hill is the author of an autobiography: *Up From Loehmann's: One Black Girl's Struggle*.

As you read, consider the following questions:

1. What is the origin of the word "mulatto," according to Fales-Hill?
2. How did Fales-Hill first learn about her parents' racial difference?
3. What is "Black Princess Guilt," according to the author?

Reprinted from "Upfront: My Life in Black and White," by Susan Fales-Hill, *Vogue*, June 2000. Reprinted with permission from the author.

I'm sick in bed watching Oprah one afternoon, and I want to scream—and not because I don't like what she's wearing. A sobbing biracial girl is being comforted by a midriff-baring Mariah Carey, the Oprah-anointed pop patron saint of "mulattos." (Don't let her blonde locks fool you; Mariah is half black.) Oprah asks Mariah and the disconsolate teen if hearing about their painful experiences will confirm the public's belief that the children of mixed marriages are doomed to suffer. "That's not true!" I find myself shouting at the screen. "Why didn't you ask me or any of my well-adjusted mixed friends?! I'm living proof that mixed does not mean mixed up! I'm doing fine!" (If that's true, why am I yelling at a television screen in the middle of the afternoon? you may ask.) So often have I heard people assume that being "mixed" is tantamount to misery, and so desperate am I to share my message of hope with the world that I briefly consider climbing up to my rooftop to shout it out. But since I live in a respectable Park Avenue co-op, right across the street from the Lenox Hill Hospital mental ward, I reconsider my approach.

We "mulattos" (I put the word in quotation marks because it comes from the Spanish word for *mules)* have always gotten bad PR. We've been denounced as Satan's spawn. To quote an old American adage: "God made the black man, and God made the white man, but the Devil made the mulatto." We've been ridiculed in literature (e.g., the bimboish "woolly haired mulatto from Saint Kitts" in Thackeray's *Vanity Fair)*. And made to seem pathetic in the movies (e.g., the self-loathing, light-skinned, mulatto-looking daughter in *Imitation of Life* who publicly rejects her dark-skinned mother, only to throw herself sobbing on her mother's casket at her funeral). Then there's the brilliant question I'm often asked: "Your mother's black and your father's white. So what does that make you?" Human, last time I checked.

A Quintessentially American Story

Contrary to popular belief, being born into a biracial home does not automatically condemn one to a life of isolation and ethnic schizophrenia, "torn between two races, feeling like a café au lait fool." (Just ask Tiger Woods.) For me, growing up biracial has been a privilege and an extraordinary adventure. My story may not be typical, but it is in a sense quintessentially American, and with its melding of immigrant, Afro-Caribbean, Puritan, and European cultures, quintessentially African-American. (Didn't anyone else watch *Sally Hemings: An American Scandal*, the miniseries on Thomas Jefferson's black mistress?)

My parents wed in 1958, when the anti-miscegenation laws still on the books rendered their marriage illegal in many states. (In Virginia, they would have been imprisoned. So much for that honeymoon jaunt to Colonial Williamsburg!) My mother, the daughter of Haitian political exiles, was a singer and actress appearing on Broadway in the musical *Jamaica* with Lena Horne. My father, scion of a WASP Brahmin family (some ancestors came on the *Mayflower*; others caught the "second boat"), worked as an executive at a shipping company. A mutual friend, Johnny Galliher, took my father to see the show. As my mother belted out the show-stopping number "Leave de Atom Alone," my father decided he would never leave *her* alone. At the end of the performance, he said to his friend, "That's the mother of my children." Two months and scores of roses later, my mother agreed to a date. They were married April 15 of that year by legendary minister/politician Adam Clayton Powell, Jr. Their marriage caused shock waves in New York: Timothy Fales, son of DeCoursey Fales, commodore of the New York Yacht Club, marrying Josephine Premice, a *colored woman in show business!* . . .

Learning the Racial Facts of Life

I first realized my parents were different "colors" when I was five. I had spent the day with my father and was astonished at his mystical power over the city's taxis. He had only to raise his hand in the air and the lemon-yellow vehicles would come screeching to a halt. This to my childish eyes was akin to the parting of the Red Sea on the scale of miracles. I felt certain my father was a magician. It was so different from being out with Mommie. Three or four Checker cabs (yes, they had them then) would speed past us before even one would stop. Or the OFF DUTY sign would suddenly illuminate when we came into view. Upon arriving home, I announced to my mother, "Papa's really good at getting cabs, and you're terrible." That was the first time my mother sat me down to explain the racial facts of life in America in 1968. The cabdrivers didn't want to pick her up, she explained, because she was black and they thought she was going to Harlem or some other "undesirable" neighborhood. Papa was white. They assumed he was going someplace nice. Though I've never forgotten that moment, it was far from devastating. Mommie presented the injustice to me as part of an ugly but not immutable status quo, like slavery, or her own experiences singing in clubs she couldn't attend as a patron in the fifties. Her message was one of hope. There was nothing wrong with us; it was society that was tragically misinformed. My brother Enrico and I had a responsibility to help the "blind" see.

An Empowering Identity

I have no desire to deny my blackness. To deny my blackness is to deny my mother, my grandparents, my aunts and uncles, and cousins who have undoubtedly contributed to the person that I am. Likewise, to deny that I am also white, is to deny my father, my grandparents, my aunts and uncles and my cousins who have supported me every day throughout my life.

Indeed, I have no need to deny any part of my family to "fit in." Further, this [racial] ambiguity has provided me with a wonderful sense of empowerment concerning my identity. My identity is constantly being defined by everything other than my perceived race.

Kenya Mayfield, *Interrace*, January 1996.

In spite of the racial turmoil and upheaval of the period, our life was relatively free of strife. My brother and I were fully accepted in both our families. We spent many an evening with our Haitian grandfather, Lucas Premice, in his Brooklyn brownstone. We would listen to his diatribes (in French and Creole) against the Duvaliers while feasting on codfish fritters, roast pork, rice with Haitian dark wild mushrooms (dubbed Black Power Rice by my aunts), and the best crème caramel on earth. In the winter, we had Sunday lunches of roast beef and Yorkshire pudding at Grandma Fales's town house on East Seventy-second. Ancestral portraits peered down at us from the red damask walls of the dining room. The faces were not forbidding; they smiled. They seemed neither shocked nor outraged at the turn the family tree had taken. Though goodness knows, it was unexpected for these august Puritans. Summers we spent on my grandmother's estate in Gladstone, New Jersey, where black people were such a rare sight that the first time my mother set foot in the local convenience store they knew immediately she was "the one who had married into the Fales family." (Each time we saw a black person in town, my parents would excitedly point him or her out. I found this odd and uncouth until they explained their elation to me. It meant things were changing.) Though my mother, with her mahogany skin, pipe-cleaner-thin body, extravagant clothes, and false eyelashes, certainly stood out among the tweedy "hunt-club set," she absolutely refused to change who she was. I can see her now striding into the vegetable garden in her stilettos, full makeup, and a spaghetti-strap chiffon gown to pick fresh tomatoes for our evening meal. "Take me as I am," she seemed to declare to the WASP world. And it did. (My grandmother, a Colonial Dame of America, accepted my mother fully. She became my grandfather's favorite daughter-in-law.) My mother's refusal to bow to someone else's standard of "correctness" taught me that I didn't have to spend my life seeking other people's acceptance or approval, that "fitting in," like virginity, was a highly overrated virtue.

Life in a Multiethnic Colony

In addition to the love of our families, we enjoyed the support of our parents' eclectic, multiethnic group of friends. In fact, we were part of a sort of ad hoc "mixed-marriage colony." Far from being oddballs, we knew many other children like us. There were Kahli and Pucci, whose mother wrote cookbooks. There were the Sandler girls. Brad Johnson, whose mother was Italian. My mother's best friend, Diahann Carroll, whose daughter, Suzanne Kaye, was half Jewish. And Harry and Julie Belafonte and their children. And when she was in town, Eartha Kitt and her daughter, Kitt

Shapiro. We ranged in color from chocolate-brown to fair, with blonde hair and green eyes. This didn't strike any of us as odd. No one ever said, "So-and-so doesn't look black." To us, *black* didn't denote one particular shade or manner of behaving but rather an infinite kaleidoscope of possibilities.

My brother and I attended the Lycée Français de New York. The atmosphere was on the *Tom Brown Schooldays* side of Draconian, but the student body was wonderfully diverse. It was hard to feel like an "other" when you were surrounded by everyone from Tunisians to Vietnámese to Senegalese to Belgians to Yugoslavians. My parents dealt with the stereotyping in popular culture by creating a cult of "uniqueness." When Farrah Fawcett-Majors appeared, wiggling and jiggling on television, my mother would say, "Anyone can look like her; you look different, and that's wonderful.". . .

Though white, my father had an encyclopedic knowledge of black culture internationally. . . . More so than any professor, he showed me the interconnectedness of all the world's cultures, whether it was in the person of Alexander Pushkin (the Russian writer of Abyssinian descent) or the decor of our home, in which a Malian sculpture might sit on a Hepplewhite table. My father was also far from naive about the challenges my brother and I would face. He didn't treat us like white children with a tan. Our parents explained that though we had a claim to both our heritages, America would classify us as black. And that was just fine because, whether or not America realized it, black was beautiful, varied, rich, and noble.

Belonging Everywhere and Nowhere

Harvard proved my real dose of being judged by the color of my skin rather than the content of my character. I didn't know I was "fair-skinned." I didn't know I was supposed to sit at the Freshman Black Table to prove what I already knew: that I was not and never would be white. Many of the black students assumed I identified only with the culture of DWMs (Dead White males) and that I would date only LWMs (Live White Males). The reaction of whites was often amusing. They would meet my very Cantabrigian uncle DeCoursey Fales, Jr., at a Fly Club function (the Fly is an exclusive all-male social club, one of several Final Clubs at Harvard) and hear him speak of his niece. Their jaws would literally drop when they realized I was that niece. I would inevitably be asked, "How is he your uncle?" (I would refer such benighted souls to Claude Lévi-Strauss's *The Elementary Structures of Kinship* or, better yet, to Webster's Dictionary.) Others were purely welcoming, such as the late John Marquand, a residential tutor who had known my father and my cousin. When I introduced myself, he didn't bat an eye but immediately made the connection.

There were days I belonged "everywhere and nowhere." When listening to certain African-American students talk about their belief in the innate racism of whites, I couldn't, for the life of me, identify. To me, the white race was not a hostile and alien monolith; it was my beloved grandmother and grandfather, my doting uncles, my cousins, my father. It was my blood. I did, however, feel equally alienated from insouciant Caucasian students who didn't believe their infractions would reflect poorly on their families or their people. They didn't know what it was to feel "When and where I enter, the whole race enters with me." Whether it was in a classroom or at a keg party, I always felt the weight of being a cultural ambassador of blacks and the offspring of mixed marriages. People teased me about my formal manner and my obsession with dressing well. I didn't have the luxury enjoyed by whites of walking around in torn jeans and being treated as an equal member of society. (My mother had drummed it into me: "We shall overcome . . . in couture!") Still, I relished my undergraduate years.

Black Princess Guilt

Growing up, I was struck by an affliction common to many young African-American women from affluent backgrounds: acute BPG—Black Princess Guilt. "I've never lived in the 'hood," goes the self-flagellating mantra. "I've only driven through it in an expensive foreign car." By definition, Black Princesses haven't struggled, or wrestled the demon Poverty. Our stories of oppression begin with lines like "There I was at the cashmere-sweater counter. . . ." These are not stories of being harassed by the police; they are stories of being treated like "less than a shopper" in expensive boutiques. And so, like many others suffering with BPG, I went out and found a boyfriend who would give me as hard a time as possible about growing up privileged. Lorenzo (name has been changed to protect the guilty), though he was also mixed, constantly berated me for being a "white girl in brownface." I couldn't sing like Mahalia Jackson or break into the vernacular. In short, I lacked *soul*. My academic achievements were all well and good, but did I know how to survive "on the street"? Well, I thought I did, but according to him, Bond Street and Madison Avenue didn't count. I was woefully unprepared for "real life." I wore this psychological hair shirt for several years, until one bright day it occurred to me that my parents were right. Being "authentically black" did not mean being authentically poor. Nor did it mean speaking fluent Ebonics or qualifying for membership in the Abyssinian Baptist Church Choir. Though Lorenzo's abdominals were chiseled to perfection, his ideas were nothing if not informed. Let's face it, in street parlance, they were *wack!* I bid him and BPG *sayonara* and began my quest for a true soul mate.

Being a Cultural Mulatto

Over the years, I dated everyone from a rapper named after a breakfast cereal to WASP trust-fund babies. With my mixed friend Suzanne Kaye, I discussed marrying black or white. At the end of the day, it came down to marrying human beings who understood us. My husband, a black American of British West Indian descent who grew up in Hanover, New Hampshire (black population: his family), knows firsthand what it means to be a cultural mulatto, to fit in everywhere and nowhere. He immediately understood my West Indian side, relished my "WASPy" side, and celebrated my European side. He doesn't, in other words, try to condense my identity.

This year in the census, for the first time, I had the opportunity of checking more than one ethnic box. I did so, not in order to set myself apart but to declare who I am. (Truth is, most African-Americans could check more than one box, and for all some whites know, so could they.) I will do so to acknowledge both of my families, and especially my parents, whose humor, love, madness, arrogance, and irreverence helped me, far more than economic privilege, to overcome the prejudices of our society. And so to those who would ask, "Your mother's black and your father's white. What does that make you?" I have only one reply: "Rich, baby."

VIEWPOINT

5

"*Given the current crisis involving the disproportionate numbers of black children in need of permanent homes, transracial adoptions should be advocated.*"

Transracial Adoptions Should Be Encouraged

Amanda T. Perez

Adoption policies that emphasize placing minority children with parents of their own race can be harmful, argues Amanda T. Perez in the following viewpoint. Minority children comprise a large percentage of youngsters in need of adoption, and they can wait years before being placed in permanent homes—which is often a hindrance to a child's emotional development, Perez points out. These children should not be required to wait the extra amount of time that it can take to find them parents of their own race, Perez insists. If no same-race parents can be found, the child should be placed with parents of another race as soon as possible. Perez is a law clerk for a United States District Court in New Jersey.

As you read, consider the following questions:
1. According to Perez, why did a federal district court return Raymond Bullard to his first foster home?
2. In what instance *should* race be considered in child placement decisions, in the author's view?
3. What percentage of children waiting to be adopted are children of color, according to Perez?

Excerpted from Amanda Perez, "Transracial Adoption and the Federal Adoption Subsidy," *Yale Law and Policy Review*, vol. 17, no. 1, pp. 201–206. Reprinted by permission of The Yale Law and Policy Review, Inc. Notes and references in the original have been omitted in this reprint.

Raymond Bullard was two and a half years old when he was removed from his foster home, where he had lived happily for two years with a white family, to be placed with a black family. Raymond was taken from the only home he had known because the Philadelphia Department of Human Services had a policy against long-term interracial foster care and adoption placements. The removal was in no way attributed to the quality of care provided by Raymond's foster parents. Two years later, Raymond was diagnosed as clinically depressed. His speech impediment had grown worse and he displayed excessive aggression and preoccupation with death. Only after this diagnosis was made did the federal district court return Raymond to his initial foster home.

Though Raymond's story is an exceptional one, it illustrates the significance race is accorded in child-placement decisions. Though no one intended to hurt Raymond, the child suffered tremendous emotional trauma as a result of the separation from his family due to concern about the color of his skin. Many children today are wallowing in unstable foster or institutional care rather than being placed with adoptive parents of another race. A child's race or cultural heritage are permissible factors for consideration in the determination of the best interests of the child. Race-matching, however, is often valued above the immediate placement of children in permanent homes. Raymond's case introduces the complicated issues that arise from the consideration of race in the best interests analysis and the resistance to transracial placements in the adoption context. . . .

A Practical Position

This essay builds upon a practical rather than idealistic position regarding the proper weight to be given to race in child placement decisions. Race and culture are indeed significant to a child's identity and affect her human experience in numerous ways. There is an intimate connection between race, culture, and identity that shapes the way the child thinks about and perceives herself, others, and the world around her. There is no doubt that a black child raised in a white family and a black child raised in a black family will have distinct experiences. It also is highly likely that a black child raised in a white family will experience, to some extent, societal pressures, confusion about identity, and tension between the two worlds to which she belongs. These additional complications exacerbate the difficulties facing all minorities in American society.

Nonetheless, given the current crisis involving the disproportionate numbers of black children in need of permanent homes, transracial adoptions should be advocated. Race should never factor into a placement determination when the result is leaving a child in foster or institutional care. If there are no same-race parents with whom to place a child, the child should be placed *immediately* with adoptive parents of a different race. Put simply, race should never preclude or delay an adoptive placement for *any* period of time.

Race should be a factor in placement decisions in only one instance—when there are qualified black and white prospective parents waiting to adopt. In this circumstance, children should be assigned on a same-race basis. Given the stark reality that black children are adopted at a lower rate than are white children, we must grapple with the difficult issue of transracial adoption when same-race parents are not immediately available. The goal in adoption should be finding immediate, permanent homes for children. Children need families in which to grow and develop in a normal, healthy manner. The choice between making a transracial placement and waiting for a black family to become available to adopt a minority child should be easy—the transracial placement should be made, and the child should be given a home and family to call her own.

The Statistical Imbalance

Both the elimination of barriers to nonminority couples' adoption of minority children and the provision of a federal adoption subsidy are useful social policies. Both facilitate the location of permanent homes for the disproportionate numbers of minority children in the foster care system. The severity of the gap in placement rates between minority and nonminority children is a driving force in the transracial adoption controversy that warrants attention. Approximately forty-seven percent of the children waiting to be adopted are of color and forty percent are categorized as black, though blacks constitute only twelve percent of the U.S. population. On average, minority children wait two years before being matched with a parent, twice as long as nonminority children.

In 1995, Senator Howard Metzenbaum found that nearly 500,000 children were in foster care in the United States. Of these children, black children waiting to be adopted waited approximately twice as long as non-black children, who waited a median length of two years and eight months. Because it is more difficult to find families willing to adopt older children, a child's chances of ever receiving a permanent placement decrease the longer a child remains in foster care.

A Fully Positive Experience

The studies of trans-racial adoptive families are extraordinarily interesting. They do not simply show that black children do well in white adoptive homes. They do not simply show that we put black children at risk by delaying or denying placement while we await black homes. The studies show that black children raised in white homes are comfortable with their blackness and also uniquely comfortable in dealing with whites. In addition, the studies show that trans-racial adoption has an interesting impact on the racial attitudes of the *white* members of these families. The parents tend to describe their lives as significantly changed and enriched by the experience of becoming an inter-racial family. They describe themselves as having developed a new awareness of racial issues. The white children in trans-racial adoptive families are described as committed to and protective of their black brothers and sisters. The white as well as the black children are described as unusually free of racial bias, and unusually committed to the vision of a pluralistic world in which one's humanity is more important than one's race.

Elizabeth Bartholet, *Reconstruction*, vol. 1, no. 4, 1992.

In 1991, the National Adoption Center's statistics revealed that 31% of families waiting to adopt were black and 67% were white. Yet a survey by the National Center for Health Statistics concluded that only 7.6% of adoptions reported by women were transracial, of which 1.2% involved a white mother and a black child. To be sure, many prospective adoptive parents are not interested in adopting across racial lines. Those who are, however, often encounter bureaucratic resistance that stems from personal or agency prejudices. These prejudices, furthermore, have been exacerbated by the continuing resistance of the National Association of Black Social Workers (NABSW) to transracial adoption. A black child's chance of being adopted has already suffered as a result of the 1972 release by the NABSW of a position statement that referred to transracial adoption as "cultural genocide." After the group announced its position, many groups shifted their policies and the number of transracial placements plummeted.

Racial Policies

Adoption agency policies often make race the central factor in the placement process. Whites who have expressed an interest in adopting older black children with significant disabilities have been turned away from public adoption agencies. Despite the need to find homes for minority children and the potentially large number of white parents wanting to adopt a child of another race, children are often shifted between foster care situations, left to remain in institutions, or subjected to unnecessary delays in permanent placements. This is due, in part, to institutional aversion to transracial adoptions. Transracial adoptions take place more frequently in private adoption agencies, where many barriers present in the state adoption process do not exist. Though public agencies are licensed by the state and run by state or city governments, there is minimal state regulation of private adoption agencies. Therefore, private agencies are free to exclude race from consideration as they make placement decisions.

Social workers and adoption agencies wield a great deal of power in the adoption process. Courts view adoption agencies as the experts at discerning what is in a child's best interest. Social workers have filled a gap "between a couple's desire to adopt and a court's ability to determine whether petitioners would indeed be adequate parents." Social workers serve as "advocate[s] for couples who want [to adopt and for women and institutions who want] to surrender their children." Some studies have revealed that a social worker's race is one of the strongest factors affecting her attitude towards transracial adoption. Black social workers disapprove of transracial adoption more often than white social workers.

Other Factors Affecting Transracial Adoption

Private biases and hostility towards transracial placements are not wholly to blame, however, for the statistical imbalance of minority children needing homes. Other factors contributing to the disproportionate numbers of minority children waiting for homes include societal perceptions of the importance of biological similarity within the family, the malleability of the law governing the consideration of race by bureaucrats, and the fact that many black adults today cannot meet the financial prerequisites adopted by the states for adopting children. The lack of guidance from the Supreme Court regarding the proper role of race in placement decisions and the lack of concrete federal law in this area also contribute to the problem. Regardless of the cause, this problem demands immediate attention.

> "*Many transracial adoptees bemoan the fact that their adoptive parents were ill-equipped to help them with [cultural and racial] issues.*"

Transracial Adoptions Should Not Be Encouraged

Leora Neal

In 1972, the National Association of Black Social Workers (NABSW) took an influential stance against transracial adoption, arguing that African-American children needed to grow up within their own culture among members of their own race. In the following viewpoint, Leora Neal clarifies this policy. Black children need black parents to learn to deal effectively with racism and to develop a healthy cultural identity and self-esteem, the NABSW maintains. Moreover, plenty of blacks wish to adopt, Neal points out—but the misguided policies of many child care agencies create barriers for these prospective parents. These barriers must be abolished, and transracial adoption should occur only when all efforts to find same-race parents fail, she concludes. Neal directs the New York chapter of the Association of Black Social Workers Child Adoption, Counseling and Referral Service.

As you read, consider the following questions:
1. According to R. Hill, cited by the author, what percentage of black children born out of wedlock are informally adopted by African Americans?
2. According to Neal, what happens to many transracial adoptees when they grow up and leave home?

Reprinted from "The Case Against Transracial Adoption," by Leora Neal, *Focal Point*, Spring 1996. Reprinted with permission from *Focal Point*.

The National Association of Black Social Workers is an international organization composed of social workers and others in related fields. The purpose of the organization is to address itself to social welfare issues effecting Black peoples no matter where they happen to reside in the world and to bring services to African-American communities. There are over one hundred chapters in the United States in addition to chapters in the Bahamas, Canada, England and affiliations with Black social workers in South Africa and other African nations.

In 1972, at its fourth annual conference, held in Memphis, Tennessee, the National Association of Black Social Workers (NABSW) issued a resolution opposing the growing practice of placing African-American children in need of adoptive homes with Caucasian parents. The resolution was not based on racial hatred or bigotry, nor was it an attack on White parents. The resolution was not based on any belief that White families could not love Black children, nor did we want African-American children to languish in foster care rather than be placed in White adoptive homes.

Our resolution, and the position paper that followed, was directed at the child welfare system that has systematically separated Black children from their birth families. Child welfare workers have historically undertaken little effort to rehabilitate African-American parents, to work with extended families, or to reunite children in foster care with their families. Further, Black families and other families of color who tried to adopt waiting children were often met with discrimination or discouragement.

The Case Against Transracial Adoption

Accordingly, the NABSW took a position against transracial adoption in order to: (1) preserve African-American families and culture; (2) enable African-American children to appreciate their culture of origin through living within a family of the same race and culture; (3) enable African-American children to learn how to cope with racism through living with families who experience racism daily and have learned to function well in spite of that racism; and (4) to break down the systemic barriers that make it difficult for African-American and other families of color to adopt.

This position forced child care agencies to examine their policies and helped to highlight the inequities in the child welfare system that did not give African-Americans equal access to African-American children. It also made agencies take into consideration the concept of the importance of maintaining the child's culture and heritage of origin. However, they did not always take the next step in consistently accessing the African-American community in order to recruit Black families. Further, African-American families are often discouraged, discriminated against, or "screened out" of the adoption process because of cultural misunderstandings, racist attitudes, and ethnocentrism on the part of staff, as well as economic factors (such as high fees, low income). Studies such as *Barriers to Same Race Placement* (1991) conducted by the North American Council on Adoptable Children and Festinger's 1972 study, *Why Some Choose Not to Adopt Through Agencies* attest to these facts. The 1986 Westat Incorporated *Adoptive Services for Waiting Minority and Non-Minority Children* study showed that when the Black community perceived that a child care agency was welcoming toward African-Americans, the agency had no problem making adoptive placements within the community. On the other hand, if the community perceived a child care agency as not being "user friendly" they would not patronize the agency.

Barriers to Same Race Placement also revealed that agencies run by African-Americans were successful in placing 94% of their Black child population with African-American families. Child care agencies who are having difficulty working with the African-American community need to consult with Black-run agencies to learn their successful strategies. Among others, the success of the Association of Black Social Workers' Child Adoption, Counseling and Referral Service (New York Chapter), Homes for Black Children (Detroit), the Institute for Black Parents (Los Angeles), Roots, Inc. (Georgia), and the One Church One Child Program (nationwide), have dispelled the myth that Black families do not adopt.

Adoption has always been part of the culture of Black people in Africa, the United States and in the Caribbean. Transracial placements are simply not necessary for the majority of Black children available for adoption. R. Hill's study *Informal Adoptions Among Black Families* (1977) revealed that 90% of African-American children born out of wedlock are informally adopted. C. Gershenson's study, *Community Response to Children Free for Adoption* (published by the U.S. Department of Health and Human Services, 1984) demonstrates that—with respect to formal adoptions through child caring agencies and the courts—African-American families adopt at a rate 4.5 times greater than any other ethnic group. If the barriers that keep thousands of African-Americans from adopting were eliminated and recruitment efforts were consistent and ongoing, Black children would be placed in African-American homes in even greater numbers.

Hill's Black Pulse Survey, conducted in 1981 and 1993, showed that there were three million African-American households interested in adoption. There are approximately 69,000 children with the goal of adoption nationwide and 43% of these children are African-American (U.S. Department of Health and Human Services, 1990). If only a fraction of the families interested in adoption were approved, there would be enough African-American families to adopt Black children.

Keeping Agencies "In Business"

Children remain in foster care rather than being returned to relatives or adopted in an expeditious manner because there is a financial disincentive to release large numbers of children. Public and some private agencies receive governmental funds of $15,000 to $100,000 per year per child. These funds, tied to the numbers of children in foster care, are used to keep the agencies in business. If large numbers of children are released at any given time and are not replaced by equal numbers of children, an agency would have to downsize or close down. Foster care has become a billion dollar industry! Private agencies that receive no governmental monies often charge high fees. Beside the fact that fees of $2,000 to $9,000 per child create a financial hardship for some families, many Black families feel that paying fees is akin to slavery (buying children) and are angered by the practice. Therefore, one-half of the Black children placed by private agencies who do not receive governmental purchase of service fees are adopted transracially.

Transracial adoptions have increased due to the shortage of White infants and toddlers available for adoption. Contrary to the popular myth, transracial adoptions will have little effect in decreasing the large numbers of children in foster care because most of the children are school-aged or are children with special needs. Only four percent of children available for adoption nationwide are infants and toddlers under the age of two (U.S. Department of Health and Human Services, 1990). However, the majority of White families who would consider a transracial adoption want infants and toddlers. There is no shortage of Black families for such children.

Black Children Need Black Parents

Researcher L. Chestang states that African American children must be taught to function in both black and white society. This dual personality, a survival skill, can only be taught by African Americans. Black children reared by responsible black parents will have learned the tools necessary to cope with America's racism. In addition, a black child raised in a black community has the option to retreat to his or her community for solace when pressures mount. Transracially adopted children, however, are oftentimes viewed as aliens in the white community and traitors in the black community. This child will have virtually no identity and will become an outcast in both communities. This has serious implications for identity formation.

Felicia Law, *Berkeley McNair Journal*, Summer 1993.

It should be noted that 44% of the children available for adoption nationwide are White (mostly school-age and/or have special needs). However, there is little discussion concerning these children and their right to a permanent home. There is no suggestion from proponents of transracial adoptions that White children who are "languishing in the system" be adopted by African-Americans or other people of color. African-American families who have tried to adopt White children have been blocked by child care agencies and the courts most of the time. Accordingly, in practice, transracial adoptions are a "one-way street." The question arises whether the thrust for increasing transracial adoptions is truly concerned with the "best interests of Black children" or "the right of [W]hite people to parent whichever child they choose?"

The Importance of Race and Culture

Adoption is supposed to be a service to children, not parents. Adult adoptees of all races state that they have a human right to know their heritages. They are demanding more openness in adoptions and are searching for their biological relatives. Children placed with families of the same culture and race suffer great loss issues due to their separation from their biological families. Children placed transracially suffer a double loss because they have lost their cultural and racial connections as well.

Many adult transracial adoptees report that, once they leave home, they feel that they do not belong anywhere. On the one hand they are not fully accepted in the White community and—even though they are more accepted in the Black community—they often do not understand various cultural nuances. Race and culture cannot be ignored. According to R. Howe, "The key to successful living as a minority person in a discrimination, denigrating society is to have positive affirmation with others like oneself, from whom one can gain support and affirmation and learn coping skills."

The National Association of Black Social Workers has first and foremost been concerned with the preservation of African-American families. Very little effort has been put forth by the child welfare system to keep families together or to return children in foster care to their relatives. It is much more economical to keep children in their families than it is to fund their foster care. Unfortunately, preventive service programs are in danger of being cut by federal, state and local governments. Children come into foster care because of poverty-related issues. To deny help to these families is to ignore their strengths and to deny the importance of strengthening African-American communities to support the positive functioning of Black children.

Therefore, in 1994 the NABSW issued a paper on preserving African-American families. This paper states the organization's current policy regarding transracial adoptions: (1) All efforts should be made to keep children with their biological relatives via preventive services or return those children who are already in foster care; (2) For those children who cannot return to relatives, adoption by a family of the same race and culture is the next best option to preserve cultural continuity; and (3) Transracial adoptions should be a last resort only after a documented failure to find an African-American home. Transracial placements should be reviewed and supported by representatives of the African-American community.

For those children who must be placed transracially, it must be remembered that White adoptive families become "mixed" families after they adopt transracially. They have to be given pre- and post-adoption services to enable them to help their children cope with racism and culture of origin disconnection. Many transracial adoptees bemoan the fact that their adoptive parents were ill-equipped to help them with these issues and that their self-esteem suffered as a result. The child welfare system must become more culturally competent and recognize that infants as well as older children grieve over their biological family and cultural losses.

The NABSW launched its Fist Full of Families Nationwide Adoption Initiative during the October 1995 Million Man March in Washington, D.C. and received over 9,000 adoption inquiries in the subsequent six months. The expression of such a volume of interest in adoption demonstrates that, for the majority of African-American children, transracial adoptions are unnecessary.

Periodical Bibliography

The following articles have been selected to supplement the diverse views presented in this chapter. Addresses are provided for periodicals not indexed in the *Readers' Guide to Periodical Literature*, the *Alternative Press Index*, the *Social Sciences Index*, or the *Index to Legal Periodicals and Books*.

Erin Bannister — "The Meaning of Mulatto," *Essence*, August 1998.

Myrna Allen Cook — "Why I Married a White Man," *Ebony*, March 1999.

Ellis Cose — "Our New Look: The Colors of Race," *Newsweek*, January 1, 2000.

Michael A. Fletcher — "Interracial Marriages Eroding Barriers," *Washington Post*, December 28, 1998.

Lise Funderburg — "Who Should Adopt Our Children?" *Essence*, January 1998.

Michael Lind — "The Beige and the Black," *New York Times Magazine*, August 16, 1998.

Rose Martelli — "My Brother Is Black," *Redbook*, November 1999.

Judith Miller — "Banishing Racial Strife on the Wings of Love," *New York Times* (Late New York edition), May 23, 1998.

Esther Pan — "Why Asian Guys Are on a Roll," *Newsweek*, February 21, 2000.

Karen S. Peterson — "Interracial Dating: For Today's Teens, Race 'Not an Issue Anymore,'" *USA Today*, November 3, 1997.

Connie Rose Porter — "Something to Talk About," *Seventeen*, August 1999.

Delina D. Pryce — "Black Latina," *Hispanic*, March 1999. Available from the Hispanic Publishing Corporation, 98 San Jacinto Blvd., Ste. 1150, Austin, TX 78701.

Don Terry — "Getting Under My Skin," *New York Times Magazine*, July 16, 2000.

For Further Discussion

Chapter 1

1. Pat Buchanan and Don Feder maintain that lenient immigration policies and ethnic diversity are a threat to national unity. Does Amitai Etzioni's viewpoint effectively refute the assertions of Buchanan and Feder? Why or why not? Use evidence from the viewpoints to defend your answer.

2. Paul Craig Roberts, Deroy Murdock, and Alan Jenkins all use specific examples to help support their arguments concerning the U.S. government's system of racial classification. In your opinion, which author's use of examples is more compelling? Why?

3. Randall Kennedy argues that racial pride is misguided because it assumes that one's inherited physical features hold more significance than one's actions and deeds. Paul King disagrees, contending that feelings of racial loyalty and kinship ensure the survival of minority communities. In each viewpoint, try to find two supporting arguments that you personally agree with. Why do you agree with them?

4. Florence Wagman Roisman believes that the 1960s ideal of racial integration deserves continuing support, while Samuel Francis argues that integration as a social policy—particularly in the realm of education—is a failure. In your view, does Francis present an accurate assessment of the results of racial integration? Why or why not? Use evidence from the text to support your answer.

Chapter 2

1. William Booth reports that America's changing ethnic makeup—fueled by immigration—is creating divisive social and cultural tensions in the population. Bill Clinton contends that immigration benefits America's culture and economy. What evidence does each author present to support his conclusion? Whose argument is more persuasive? Explain.

2. Maria Hsia Chang claims that Mexican-American separatism, fueled by immigration and multiculturalism, is likely to intensify ethnic conflict in the United States. Mike Davis and Alessandra Moctezuma argue that Anglo xenophobia and nativism are fomenting segregation and "racial battlefields" in American cities. In your opinion, which poses more of a threat to the United

States: minority-group separatism or majority-group nativism? Support your answer with evidence from the viewpoints.

Chapter 3

1. Wilbert Jenkins asserts that affirmative action has honored the goals of the civil rights movement through policies that remedy the effects of past and ongoing discrimination against minorities. Charles T. Canady maintains that affirmative action has actually undermined the original purpose of the civil rights movement by fostering discriminatory racial preferences. In your view, which of these authors presents a stronger case?

2. Martin Michaelson argues that affirmative action in college admissions helps boost the ranks of qualified minority professionals and brings a healthy racial diversity to college campuses. Carl Cohen maintains that racial preference in college admissions is a form of discrimination that provokes resentment between white and nonwhite students. Michaelson is an attorney who often represents various U.S. colleges and universities; Cohen is a University of Michigan professor who has served on that university's admissions committees. Does knowing their backgrounds influence your assessment of their arguments? Explain your answer.

3. The editors of the *Brookings Review* and Alan Jenkins have differing views on how most Americans really feel about affirmative action. On what points do these authors agree? On what points do they disagree?

Chapter 4

1. Randall Kennedy promotes interracial marriage because he believes it can curb racism. Eric Liu, on the other hand, maintains that an increase in interracial marriage will not, in itself, bridge racial divides. Which author do you agree with? Why?

2. Marta I. Cruz-Janzen explains that biracial children often feel like social outcasts, torn between two cultures that are unwilling to accept their dual identity. Susan Fales-Hill writes that being biracial, while not trouble-free, is a "privilege and an extraordinary adventure." In your opinion, what accounts for the difference of opinion that these authors have about growing up biracial? Explain.

Organizations to Contact

The editors have compiled the following list of organizations concerned with the issues debated in this book. The descriptions are derived from materials provided by the organizations. All have publications or information available for interested readers. The list was compiled on the date of publication of the present volume; the information provided here may change. Be aware that many organizations take several weeks or longer to respond to inquiries, so allow as much time as possible.

American Immigration Control Foundation (AICF)
PO Box 525
Monterey, VA 24465
(703) 468-2022 • fax: (703) 468-2024

The AICF is a research and educational organization whose primary goal is to promote a reasonable immigration policy based on national interests and needs. The foundation educates the public on what its members believe are the disastrous effects of uncontrolled immigration. It publishes the monthly newsletter *Border Watch* as well as several monographs and books on the historical, legal, and demographic aspects of immigration.

Center for the Study of Biracial Children
2300 S. Krameria St., Denver, CO 80222
(303) 692-9008
e-mail: francis@csbc.cncfamily.com
website: www.csbc.cncfamily.com

The Center for the Study of Biracial Children produces and disseminates materials for and about interracial families and biracial children. The center provides advocacy, training, and consulting. *Tomorrow's Children*, by Dr. Francis Wardle, one of the foremost authorities on multiethnic identity, can be ordered at the center's website.

Center for the Study of Popular Culture (CSPC)
9911 W. Pico Blvd., Suite 1290, Los Angeles, CA 90035
(310) 843-3699 • fax: (310) 843-3692
website: www.cspc.org

CSPC is a conservative educational organization that addresses topics such as political correctness, cultural diversity, and discrimination. Its civil rights project promotes equal opportunity for all individuals and provides legal assistance to citizens challenging affirmative action. The center publishes four magazines: *Heterodoxy, Defender, Report Card,* and *COMINT.*

Center for the Study of White American Culture
245 W. 4th Ave., Roselle, NJ 07203
(908) 241-5439
e-mail: contact@euroamerican.org
website: www.euroamerican.org

The center is a multiracial organization that supports cultural exploration and self-discovery among white Americans. It also encourages dialogue among all racial and cultural groups concerning the role of white American culture in the larger American society. It publishes the Whiteness Papers series, including "Decentering Whiteness" and "White Men and the Denial of Racism."

Citizens' Commission on Civil Rights (CCCR)
2000 M St. NW, Suite 400, Washington, DC 20036
(202) 659-5565 • fax: (202) 223-5302
e-mail: citizens@cccr.org • website: www.cccr.org

CCCR monitors the federal government's enforcement of antidiscrimination laws and promotes equal opportunity for all. It publishes reports on affirmative action and desegregation as well as the book *One Nation Indivisible: The Civil Rights Challenge for the 1990s.*

4C Cross Cultural Couples & Children
PO Box 8, Plainsboro, NJ 08536
(609) 275-9352
e-mail: tango-sierra@geocities.com
website: www.geocities.com/Heartland/Meadows/7936/7936.html

4C is a nonprofit support group committed to helping cross-cultural couples as well as children and adults of mixed racial backgrounds. The organization promotes public acceptance of interracial couples and mixed-race individuals, studies problems unique to interracial relationships, and aids in the development of self-esteem in mixed-race individuals. It publishes the quarterly newsletter *Happenings.*

Hispanic Policy Development Project (HPDP)
1001 Connecticut Ave. NW, Suite 901, Washington, DC 20036
(202) 822-8414 • fax: (202) 822-9120

HPDP encourages the analysis of public policies affecting Hispanics in the United States, particularly the education, training, and employment of Hispanic youth. It publishes a number of books and pamphlets, including *Together Is Better: Building Strong Partnerships Between Schools and Hispanic Parents*.

Interracial Family Circle (IFC)

PO Box 53291, Washington, DC 20009
(800) 500-9040 • (202) 393-7866
e-mail: ifcweb@hotmail.com
website: www.geocities.com/heartland/estates/4496

The Interracial Family Circle strives to protect and advance the rights of interracial/multicultural individuals and families through educational programs. It provides support and community for its members by offering social events. *The Collage*, IFC's newletter, and a recommended reading list of multiethnic books are available at its website.

National Association for the Advancement of Colored People (NAACP)

4805 Mt. Hope Dr., Baltimore, MD 21215-3297
(410) 358-8900 • fax: (410) 486-9257
website: www.naacp.org

The NAACP is the oldest and largest civil rights organization in the United States. Its principle objective is to ensure the political, educational, social, and economic equality of minorities. It publishes the magazine *Crisis* ten times a year as well as a variety of newsletters, books, and pamphlets.

National Association for the Advancement of White People (NAAWP)

PO Box 1727, Callahan, FL 32011
(904) 766-2253 • (813) 274-4988 • fax: (904) 924-0716
e-mail: naawp1@mediaone.net • website: www.naawp.org

NAAWP is a nonviolent civil rights organization that advocates white rights. It perceives Caucasians as being discriminated against in favor of special interest minority groups. The association, which seeks to preserve a white heritage, discourages interracial relationships. Their newsletter, *NAAWP News*, is published 8–10 times a year.

National Network for Immigrant and Refugee Rights (NNIRR)

310 Eighth St., Suite 307, Oakland, CA 94607
(510) 465-1984 • fax: (510) 465-1885
e-mail: nnirr@igc.apc.org. • website: http://www.nnirr.org

The network includes community, church, labor, and legal groups committed to the cause of equal rights for all immigrants. These groups work to end discrimination and unfair treatment of illegal immigrants and refugees. It publishes a monthly newsletter, *Network News*.

National Urban League
120 Wall St., 8th Fl., New York, NY 10005
(212) 558-5300 • fax: (212) 344-5332
website: www.nul.org

A community service agency, the National Urban League aims to eliminate institutional racism in the United States. It also provides services for minorities who experience discrimination in employment, housing, welfare, and other areas. It publishes the report *The Price: A Study of the Costs of Racism in America* and the annual *State of Black America*.

Poverty and Race Research Action Council (PRRAC)
3000 Connecticut Ave. NW, Suite 200, Washington, DC 20008
(202) 387-9887 • fax: (202) 387-0764
e-mail: info@prrac.org • website: www.prrac.org

The Poverty and Race Research Action Council is a nonpartisan, national, not-for-profit organization convened by major civil rights, civil liberties, and anti-poverty groups. PRRAC's purpose is to link social science research to advocacy work in order to successfully address problems at the intersection of race and poverty. Its bimonthly publication, *Poverty and Race*, often includes articles on race- and income-based inequities in the United States.

United States Commission on Civil Rights
624 Ninth St. NW, Suite 500, Washington, DC 20425
(202) 376-7533 • publications: (202) 376-8128

A fact-finding body, the commission reports directly to Congress and the president on the effectiveness of equal opportunity laws and programs. A catalog of its numerous publications can be obtained from its Publication Management Division.

Bibliography of Books

Teja Arboldea

In the Shadow of Race: Growing Up as a Multiethnic, Multicultural, and "Multiracial" American. Mahwah, NJ: Lawrence Erlbaum, 1998.

James A. Banks

An Introduction to Multicultural Education. Boston: Allyn and Bacon, 1999.

William G. Bowen and and Derek Curtis Bok

The Shape of the River: Long-Term Consequences of Considering Race in College and University Admissions. Princeton, NJ: Princeton University Press, 1998.

Jim Carnes

Us and Them: A History of Intolerance in America. New York: Oxford University Press, 1999.

Leslie G. Carr

"Color-Blind" Racism. Thousand Oaks, CA: Sage, 1997.

Farai Chideya

The Color of Our Future. New York: William Morrow, 1999.

Ellis Cose

Color-Blind: Seeing Beyond Race in a Race-Obsessed World. New York: HarperCollins, 1997.

George E. Curry, ed.

The Affirmative Action Debate. Reading, MA: Addison-Wesley, 1996.

Richard Delgado

When Equality Ends: Stories About Race and Resistance. Boulder, CO: Westview Press, 1999.

J. Lawrence Driskill

Cross-Cultural Marriages and the Church: Living the Global Neighborhood. Carroll Stream, IL: Hope, 1995.

Dinesh D'Souza

The End of Racism: Principles for a Multiracial Society. New York: Free Press, 1995.

Jennifer L. Eberhardt and Susan T. Fiske, eds.

Confronting Racism: The Problem and the Response. Thousand Oaks, CA: Sage, 1998.

Joe R. Feagin and Hernan Vera

White Racism: The Basics. New York: Routledge, 1995.

Martha Hodes, ed.

Sex, Love, Race: Crossing Boundaries in North American History. New York: New York University Press, 1999.

Kevin R. Johnson

How Did You Get to Be Mexican?: A White/Brown Man's Search for Identity. Philadelphia: Temple University Press, 1999.

Kathleen Odell Korgen

From Black to Biracial: Transforming Racial Identity Among Americans. Westport, CT: Praeger, 1998.

Jane Lazarre	*Beyond the Whiteness of Whiteness: Memoir of a White Mother of Black Sons*. Durham, NC: Duke University Press, 1996.
Robert G. Lee	*Orientals: Asian Americans in Popular Culture*. Philadelphia: Temple University Press, 1999.
Eric Liu	*The Accidental Asian: Notes of a Native Speaker*. New York: Random House, 1998.
Don C. Locke	*Increasing Multicultural Understanding: A Comprehensive Model*. Thousand Oaks, CA: Sage, 1998.
Kevin Luttery and Tonyan Martin, eds.	*A Stranger in My Bed*. South Orange, NJ: Bryant and Dillon, 1997.
Paula Mitchell Marks	*In a Barren Land: American Indian Dispossession and Survival*. New York: William Morrow, 1998.
Elizabeth Martinez	*De Colores Means All of Us: Latina Views for a Multi-Colored Century*. Cambridge, MA: South End Press, 1998.
Laughlin McDonald	*The Rights of Racial Minorities*. New York: Puffin, 1998.
Robert P. McNamara, Maria Tempenis, and Beth Walton	*Crossing the Line*. Westport, CT: Greenwood, 1999.
Stephen Grant Meyer	*As Long As They Don't Move Next Door: Segregation and Racial Conflict in American Neighborhoods*. New York: Rowman and Littlefield, 2000.
Scott Minerbrook	*Divided to the Vein: A Journey into Race and Family*. Orlando, FL: Harcourt Brace, 1996.
Renea D. Nash	*Coping with Interracial Dating*. New York: Rosen, 1997.
Larry L. Naylor	*American Culture: Myth and Reality of a Culture of Diversity*. Westport, CT: Bergin & Garvey, 1998.
David Palumbo-Liu	*Asian/American: Historical Crossings of a Racial Frontier*. Stanford, CA: Stanford University Press, 1999.
Elaine Pascoe	*Racial Prejudice: Why Can't We Overcome?* Danbury, CT: Franklin Watts, 1997.
Richard J. Payne	*Getting Beyond Race: The Changing American Culture*. Boulder, CO: Westview Press, 1998.
Patricia Raybon	*My First White Friend: Confessions on Race, Love, and Forgiveness*. New York: Penguin, 1997.

Maria P.P. Root, ed.   *The Multiracial Experience: Racial Borders as the New Frontier*. Newbury Park, CA: Sage, 1996.

Judy Scales-Trent   *Notes of a White Black Woman: Race, Color, Community*. University Park: Pennsylvania State University Press, 1995.

Alvin J. Schmidt   *The Menace of Multiculturalism: Trojan Horse in America*. Westport, CT: Praeger, 1997.

David K. Shipler   *A Country of Strangers: Blacks and Whites in America*. New York: Knopf, 1997.

Rita J. Simon, Howard Alstein, and Marygold S. Melli   *The Case for Transracial Adoption*. Washington, DC: American University Press, 1994.

Shelby Steele   *A Dream Deferred: The Second Betrayal of Black Freedom in America*. New York: HarperCollins, 1998.

Leonard Steinhorn and Barbara Diggs-Brown   *By the Color of Our Skin: The Illusion of Integration and the Reality of Race*. New York: Penguin, 1999.

Roberto Suro   *Strangers Among Us: How Latino Immigration Is Transforming America*. New York: Knopf, 1998.

Beverly Daniel Tatum   *"Why Are All the Black Kids Sitting Together in the Cafeteria?" and Other Conversations About Race*. New York: BasicBooks, 1997.

Ronald L. Taylor   *Minority Families in the United States: A Multicultural Perspective*. Upper Saddle River, NJ: Prentice-Hall, 1998.

Stephan Thernstrom and Abigail Thernstrom   *America in Black and White: One Nation, Indivisible*. New York: Simon and Schuster, 1997.

James Waller   *Face to Face: The Changing State of Racism Across America*. New York: Insight Books, 1998.

Tom Wicker   *Tragic Failure: Racial Integration in America*. New York: William Morrow, 1996.

Patricia J. Williams   *Seeing a Color-Blind Future: The Paradox of Race*. New York: Noonday Press, 1998.

Joel Williamson   *New People: Miscegenation and Mulattoes in the United States*. Baton Rouge: Louisiana State University Press, 1995.

Robert J.C. Young   *Colonial Desire: Hybridity in Theory, Culture, and Race*. New York: Routledge, 1995.

Index

218

221

Tocqueville, Alexis De, 175
Torres, Art, 99

University of Texas v. Hopwood, 140

Venter, Craig, 16
Villa, Pancho, 105
Voting Rights Act of 1965, 52, 116, 128
Voz Fronteriza (Chicano student newspaper), 96

Waldinger, Roger, 82
Wallace, George, 126
Wall Street Journal (newspaper), 34
War on Drugs
  has been shifted to Mexican border, 105–106
War on Poverty
  affirmative action as part of, 116
Washington, Harold, 57
Washington Civil Rights Initiative, 34
Wasserman, Satra, 12
Watanabe, Paul, 26
"We're All Minorities" (Riche), 24
Westerman, William, 26
White, Walter, 171
whites
  affirmative action does not harm,
  119–21
  in college admissions, 137
    con, 150–51
  are recipients of preferential treatment, 118
  in civil rights struggle, 50, 52
Why Some Choose to Adopt Through Agencies (Festinger), 203
Wilcox, Nathaniel J., 82, 83
Wilkins, Robert, 41
Wilkins, Roy, 130
Williams, Armstrong, 117
Wilson, August, 56
Wilson, Pete, 39
Winfrey, Oprah, 187
Wolfe, Alan, 157
women
  genital mutilation of, 20
Woods, Tiger, 13
Wright, Bobby E., 56
Wright, Richard, 171

xenophobia
  fear is at the core of, 108

Young, Whitney, 129

Zangwill, Israel, 75
Zinn, Howard, 66